Praise for *ARMS OUT*

"Though I met Kris years before he and his billboards became a household name, his curiosity, drive and an absolute refusal to do things the way they'd always been done made him stand out from the crowd. More importantly, he's a wonderfully generous person who cares deeply about making the people around him better. I'm grateful to call him a friend, and hopeful that this book will both inspire others and help them see Kris as I do."

—**MIKE PATON**, Author, Keynote Speaker
and EOS Implementer

"Once you know Kris Lindahl's story like I do, you'll want to root for him, not against him. He's faced a lot of adversity in his life, and he's always found a way to transcend it. Hopefully this book will inspire others to do the same."

—**RYAN NELSON**, Founder, Modern Artifact

ARMS OUT

Also by Kris Lindahl

Guaranteed Cash Offer:
Sell Your Property Fast With
Total Convenience and No Commissions
2024

SOLD!
Expert Advice on How to Pocket More
Money on Your Home Sale
2017

KRIS LINDAHL

ARMS OUT

My journey from hardship to household name — and what you can learn from it

For Victoria

You are everything to me — my lodestar, the person who grounds me, focuses my priorities and brings meaning to my days. I keep this photo from your first day of kindergarten in several places so I can see it often. It helps me slow down and enjoy life. It reminds me why I do what I do. It inspires me to be a great father. And most of all, it brings me joy. Every time I drop you off at school or a soccer game, I say "be the leader." And nothing makes me happier than seeing you becoming one a little more every day. I love you!

Want to live a more Arms Out life? You're not alone! Use the QR code below to register for our FREE newsletter. It's a great way to take your inspiration to the next level.

Contents

Foreword

By Cesar "C.J." Castillejos

THE PACKAGE ARRIVED as I was still grieving the sudden death of my older brother, Carlo. Carlo had suffered cardiac arrest while playing pickleball — a sport he picked up during the pandemic — leaving behind a wife and two young sons. My parents and older sister were devastated. I felt lost without my big brother. I still couldn't believe he was gone.

The package was from a good friend of mine whom I'd known since we were teenagers. I wasn't surprised that he had sent something, but I couldn't imagine what it was. When I opened it, I saw a full pickleball set: four paddles and 12 balls.

What am I going to do with these? I thought. Carlo and my older sister, Tina, were the racket sports players in the family. I was a basketball guy. Then, as I fumbled through the box of paddles and balls, I saw the note from Kris Lindahl:

Carlo would have wanted you to start playing, so let's go!

That's so Kris, I thought. He lifted me up when I really needed it, and he was pushing me to find strength in the midst of my struggle. Kris wasn't afraid of my pain. He felt it, stepped into it and walked through it with me. He and I started playing pickleball at the park where Carlo played. We still do. Every time, we know it's a tribute to my big bro.

I've known Kris since high school. Some people see those years as the "glory days," but they can be filled with cliques and divisions — people separating themselves by age, race, class and interests. As one of the few non-white kids at our school, I was aware of these walls and barriers, and I navigated life with care and caution.

But I never had to worry or wonder about Kris. He was well liked by his peers. We had a mutual respect, and we shared some common friends. Kris didn't see boundaries, so he was a natural connector. He came from a humble family background, so he didn't look down on people. He confidently knew himself, so he never felt the need to perform for others.

Kris was also a great athlete. From watching him on the football field, I knew he was a star wide receiver. And as his teammate on the court and in the locker room, I knew that he was also a solid basketball player. That's where he and I began to foster our friendship.

I was a junior. Kris was a sophomore who got moved up to varsity. Right away, I saw his competitive fire and drive to succeed. He didn't back down to upperclassmen, and he never feared a challenging matchup. He knew his talents and potential, but he also knew his role. He wasn't an aggressive, "in your face" leader. He led by working hard and pushing others to follow. He motivated you to raise your game.

Kris was a great teammate because he was grounded. He

didn't feel the need to prove anything to anyone. On the football field or basketball court, Kris wasn't about Kris. He was confident in himself and his abilities, and he simply worked hard and did his best so the *team* could win.

Today, Kris' drive for his team to win has grown even stronger. I know because he eventually invited me to join a different kind of team. I had moved back to Minnesota after finishing college in Santa Barbara, California, and I had started working with a faith-based youth-mentoring organization called Young Life. There, I walked alongside middle and high school kids as they navigated the ups, downs and all-arounds of being a teenager. Knowing how passionate Kris was about helping people in need, I invited him to our annual fundraising banquets. Year after year, he showed his support by investing in our work and offering insights on how Young Life could keep growing.

After playing pickleball with Kris one day, I ran into a group of my high school students playing basketball at the park. I checked in with each of them to make sure everything was good, then I ran into some parents of other familiar students and gave them a quick wave. Kris noticed these interactions and recognized some of the kids from our banquets. When we got back to the parking lot, he said something that completely caught me off guard.

"Whatever you're doing here, I want you to do for my company," he said. "If you can change a city with volunteers, I know you can help my team."

This was the fall of 2020, and Kris knew the pandemic was going to present huge challenges for his business and the larger community. But, as innovators often do, he focused on the opportunities instead of the obstacles. He created a role that would tap into my talents, leverage my experience and help his company navigate the uncertainties ahead.

Kris was inviting me to be his teammate once again. But on this team, I wouldn't be his point guard; I would be his Chief Culture and Community Officer. In that role, I would focus on two things: Internally, I would build a healthy team culture by serving as a life coach for agents and employees, helping them be their best selves personally and professionally. Externally, I would research local nonprofits and causes that the company could volunteer for and support.

I was happy to team up with Kris again, and I gladly took the position. I loved the fact that he wanted to build a winning team and was willing to think outside the box to do it.

Then, over the next several months, I saw Kris act differently than any other business leader I knew. While others paused to let the pandemic storm pass, he stepped into the challenge. While others laid people off, he created opportunities. He bought video equipment to communicate remotely with his team. He ramped up his company's virtual capabilities so people could navigate home buying and selling in a socially distant world. He bought gift cards and changed his billboards to help local businesses stay afloat. And he created and invested in a corporate role — mine — whose sole purpose was to help others inside and outside his organization.

Kris thrives in a crisis. Instead of complaining, blaming or making excuses, he stays positive and seeks solutions. When he finds one, he doesn't hoard it; he shares it. He has a heart to help others, and that's why his iconic Arms Out image is so authentic. It captures *who* he is and *how* he lives his life. When runners win a race, they extend their arms (Kris is a winner). When someone is overcome with joy, they fling their arms out (Kris is filled with joy).

Arms Out is about being open and saying "yes," and that's how Kris lives his life. He's open to receive, learn, let go and give away. Kris makes me think of "open arms" not because of his marketing, but because he finds his strength by embracing struggle. As you'll see in this book, he didn't raise his fists to fight his way through life. He put his arms out to embrace his hardships and help others through theirs — myself included.

If you don't know Kris like I do, then I can understand how you might think *Kris is only about Kris.* When you put your name and face (and arms) everywhere, it's easy for people to assume that you're "all about yourself." But before you start this book, I want you to understand something: Kris is *not* about himself. He's built a powerful personal brand because it opens doors for others. It helps his customers sell their homes. It enables his agents to make a living and support their families. And it creates a powerful platform for him to help others in the community. This book recounts Kris' journey, but its intention is to help you navigate *yours.*

I'll leave you with one more story about my friend Kris:

A few weeks before my brother Carlo passed, he gave me a highlight reel of my high school basketball years. He'd made it by digitizing some old 8mm videotapes, and one particular clip stood out. The game was tied 68–68 with 8 seconds left.

Our coach had drawn up a play to get the ball to our best scorer, Ryan. But after Kris dribbled up the court, he went off script. He didn't pass the ball to Ryan, as our coach wanted (and the other team expected). Nor did he take the shot himself. Instead, he passed it to the player with the best open shot: me.

I was open because I hadn't scored a single point in that game. No one expected me to have the ball when everything was on the line, especially me. But with time running out, I drove to the hoop, put up a shot and boom! It went in, just beating the buzzer.

All the attention went to me. I was the hero to our friends and fans. But I knew what had really happened: I made the winning shot, but Kris made the winning *decision*. He did what was best for the team, and we all won. It was a Kris Lindahl Arms Out moment.

As you read this book, know that the person writing it is more than a two-dimensional image on a banner ad, TV commercial, yard sign or billboard. Behind the billboard is a genuine guy who truly walks the walk. I've had a front-row seat to Kris' life, and I've seen how he shows up as an entrepreneur, marketer, teacher, teammate, father and philanthropist. But I'm most proud to know him as a friend.

I'm so glad Kris has written this book to help people discover their core values and live an Arms Out life in service to others. After you turn the last page, I hope you'll feel as inspired as I do every day.

Introduction

I.

AS I STROLL to my locker in late March 1998, I have no idea that I'm seconds away from my life changing forever. I'm 16 years old, and after moving seven times and going through a revolving door of schools and friends, I'm finally hitting my stride. I'm the starting point guard on the basketball team and a standout wide receiver on the football team. Colleges are recruiting me. Girls are noticing me. Life is better than it's been in a long time.

Then my pager buzzes.

It's my mom, and there's a "911" after her number. I've never gotten a 911 page before. Something must be up at home, but I can't know what it is until I get there.

When I push open the door and see my mother's pale face,

I know something horrible has happened.

"Your dad's been in an accident," she says. That's all I get. She and my dad have been separated for years. His alcoholism has gotten so bad that I've cut off all contact with him. Did he get in a car accident while driving drunk? Was he okay? Nobody knows the details, including my mom.

When I enter the hospital, the mood is more somber than urgent. Before we can find Dad's room, an adult arm stops me.

"Stop right there," my great-uncle Bob says. "You don't want to remember your father this way."

Uncle Bob is one of the few male role models I've had in my life to this point. He's a former Marine and labor union president. He's been around the block and doesn't pull any punches. I understand what he's trying to tell me: My dad is either dead or close to it, and he's been disfigured in some way.

Stay here or find his room? I debate my options.

I look at Uncle Bob's face one more time. Everyone else has been avoiding eye contact with me, but he stares straight into my soul.

I never see my dad again.

II.

When I learn the full story of what happened to my father, I realize that Uncle Bob's advice was one of the greatest gifts anyone has ever given me. As I would later learn in court documents, my dad and his girlfriend had been drinking all day, first at a friend's backyard barbecue, then at the bar. At some point, they got into an argument. My dad walked back to the friend's house. His girlfriend, her blood-alcohol content over twice the legal limit, jumped into his work van and drove to the house. She waited for him to exit, then drove at him. The van hit him going at least 20 mph, then dragged him over 100 feet.

My dad's death certificate reads: "Killed in a non-accidental manner from blunt-force injuries." When his body was dislodged from the undercarriage of the van, he had a crushed thorax and other mutilating injuries. He had lived for seven hours while surgeons tried to clean him internally and rebuild his shattered body. They replaced his blood supply four times. Nothing worked.

My uncle knew that the chance for me to say goodbye had already passed. Dad was gone before we got to the hospital. The hardest part was that I had already severed my relationship with him. Any possibility for reconciliation had died with him.

III.

Later that week, we're at my grandmother's house. She walks out of her bedroom holding three envelopes. One has my sister Jamie's name on it. One has my brother Kory's name on it. And one has mine. I recognize my dad's handwriting: cursive, surprisingly flowing and ornate for such a left-brained, mechanical person.

My grandmother tells us that our father wrote these letters when he found out he was being deployed abroad as a first lieutenant in the National Guard. Those were the years right after Desert Storm, and Iraq was still a hot spot. He ended up going to Norway, but at the time he assumed he was going to Baghdad or Ramadi and might never return. These are his goodbye letters.

I tear mine open and read it:

Feb. 10, 1997

Dear Kristofor:

Don't be sad, everything will be okay. I know you're going to do okay, you're an excellent athlete, all the practice & devotion shows. You are with sports like I was with my guitar when I was your age!!

I know I haven't always been the best father but I've really been trying hard since I quit drinking — please please don't ever get like I was. It doesn't get you anywhere & you miss so much you can't ever replace. Trust me, I know. I think that's all I really regret in my life — Drinking —

I've asked Grandma and Grandpa to help with my life insurance. Let them help. I know you'll be wanting a car real soon. I want you to have money for college too so please be careful.

Keep on the path you're on & you'll do well for yourself.

I will miss you.

I love you,

Dad

I give the letter to my mom and tell her to keep it. It's too hard to have it in my possession.

IV.

Fast-forward 23 years. I'm on a stage in Orlando, Florida, hosting a mastermind for real estate professionals with friend and well-known real estate leadership expert Jon Cheplak. The audience expects to hear me talk about how to scale their businesses. Kris Lindahl Real Estate has closed over $2.5 billion in its first three years, so I have some insights to share. But before I launch into my presentation, I project an enlarged image of my dad's letter on the huge screen behind me.

I look back and forth between my dad's words and the 100+ people in the audience, and I start to cry. I wanted to share the letter, but I had no idea I'd react so strongly to seeing it again. I'm still struck by Dad's regret, mostly around how his drinking affected his ability to be a good father. He wrote the words in a moment of reflection and sobriety. He stood at a crossroads. He knew he had a problem that was destroying his relationships with the people he loved. He could have turned his life around, but he went down the other path.

I keep that letter on screen for a long time so the mastermind attendees can read it as if it's been written to them. Phones slip into pockets. Laptops close. The room falls silent.

Eventually, I advance to the next slide and talk about business topics. But after the presentation, the people who shake my hand and hug me don't want to talk about real estate. Same with the people who email and text me afterwards. One of their emails reads:

"Your story really resonated with me. My father passed when I was 16. Few people understand how much it affects young men. Thank you so much for sharing your story. I loved your passion. And honestly felt like you were one of the few speakers who actually get it. Thank you!"

Why did I begin that mastermind in such a personal place? Because I've learned that internal forces stunt growth more than external ones. Entrepreneurs fixate on the economy, their competition and trends in their industry. But most people carry something locked inside that keeps them from reaching their next level of success and well-being — something painful they'd rather not share. Mine was my dad's gruesome death. I'd only recently begun to reopen that part of my life. Doing so in front of so many people felt vulnerable, but it was a huge release.

I had opened myself up to others, and they had opened themselves up to me. It was an Arms Out moment.

V.

I use the term "Arms Out" because I've become known in my markets for a certain image that has appeared on TV commercials, billboards, banner ads, yard signs, professional sports teams' Jumbotrons, and other places for several years. Stadiums filled with thousands of people have mimicked it, and video game company Activision even licensed it to promote its newest Call of Duty release in the fall of 2024.

In it, I flash a big smile with my arms extended as far as they can go. It's a positive gesture, almost childlike. But for me, it represents far more. Arms Out has become an attitude, a philosophy, a way of life. As you'll see in the pages that follow, I've experienced my share of challenges. My father's homicide was the most dramatic, but other moments could have easily sent me down the wrong path.

Resilience is baked into my personality. But family members, coaches, teachers and other guides have played a huge role in helping me avoid self-destruction. My Uncle Bob's advice to stay out of my dad's hospital room was his own Arms Out gesture to me (he literally had to put his arm out to stop me). I've tried to pay that service back to others in many ways, but never like this.

Millions of people know my face, but very few know my heart. Whenever I tell my story to colleagues, employees, students or complete strangers, they feel inspired to take leaps of their own, and I hope you will too. As I share some of the key moments of my life so far, my goal is to teach you how to make and stick to your own commitments. To open your mind. Open your heart. And most of all, open your arms to others.

Core Values

This book focuses on the experiences that have shaped me, but it's really about helping *you* take inventory of *your* life. Start by identifying the core values that drive you. Then let those values guide you through challenging situations on your way to success, however you define that word.

I'll start by sharing my own core values. Fittingly, they spell LET'S GO!:

Learning

Empathy

Tenacity

Staying Positive

Generosity

Owning It

Here's what each of those values means to me:

Learning

- Leaders are readers, and leaders are learners. I believe in relentless growth and improvement, and I value others who show a voracious curiosity.

- I'm a student first. I never stop learning or innovating.

- I love getting outside my comfort zone.

- I'm comfortable with change, I constantly adapt, and I'll do whatever it takes to get better at what I do.

Empathy

- I believe in curiosity, not judgment.

- I help people and families navigate their biggest challenges.

- I listen first, put myself in other people's shoes and meet them where they're at.

- I wake up every morning on a mission to help my neighbors.

Tenacity

- I embrace competition, and I finish what I start.

- I want the ball when the game's on the line, and I leave it all on the field.

- I find a way, never give up and outwork everyone.

- I'm both a leader and a team player.

Staying Positive

- I'm humbly confident.

- I value people who don't take themselves too seriously.

- I strive to be self-assured but also open-minded.

- I believe everyone should be secure enough to take a joke and check their ego at the door.

Generosity

- Despite the challenges I've faced, I know how lucky I am.

- I constantly donate my Time, Treasures and Talents to the communities where I live and work.

- I mentor and coach at every opportunity.

- I value generous spirits who seek out opportunities to help their neighbors — not those who have to be asked or forced to.

Owning It

- I don't make promises (or guarantees) I can't keep.

- I hold myself as accountable as I hold others, if not more.

- I value people who do what they say they're going to do.

- I'm an action-taker, not an excuse-maker.

- Don't tell me what you're going to do; show me.

The Kris Lindahl Life Timeline (So Far)

1982 ~ Kris is born in Minneapolis.

1990 ~ Kris' parents announce their separation.

1993 ~ A basketball tryout changes everything.

1998 ~ Kris' father is killed.

2008 ~ Kris graduates from Mankato State University, Minnesota.

2009 ~ Kris secures his real estate license. Kris' daughter, Victoria, is born.

2011 ~ Kris becomes the state's #1 short-sale agent.

2013 ~ Kris gives away over 2,000 mittens to local shelters and learns a valuable lesson about social media.

2014 ~ *Real Trends* ranks Kris as the #1 agent in the state.

2015 ~ Kris starts the Kris Lindahl Team.

2017 ~ The first 100 Kris Lindahl Team (KLT) billboards appear.

KLT becomes the top team at the nation's largest brokerage.

2017 ~ Kris launches his pioneering Guaranteed Cash Offer program, and changes the real estate industry forever.

2018 ~ Kris launches his own brokerage: Kris Lindahl Real Estate (KLRE).

2019 ~ Kris wins the *Business Journal*'s "40 Under 40."

2020 ~ KLRE is the #12 ranked Real Estate Mega Team in the country. (Verified by *Real Trends*)

2021 ~ KLRE is the #5 ranked Real Estate Mega Team in the country. (Verified by *Real Trends*)

2022 ~ KLRE is the #11 ranked Real Estate Mega Team in the country. (Verified by *Real Trends*)

2023 ~ KLRE is the #9 ranked Real Estate Mega Team in the country. (Verified by *Real Trends*)

2024 ~ KLRE is the #9 ranked Real Estate Mega Team in the country. Kris publishes his second best-selling book: *Guaranteed Cash Offer: Sell Your Property Fast with Total Convenience and No Commissions.*

2025 & Beyond ~ Kris stretches his arms even farther

1. Ditch Pheasants & Super Balls: A City Childhood

I WAS BORN in Northeast Minneapolis to a taxicab driver and copy machine technician. My sister, Jamie, arrived two years later. Then my brother, Kory. And later, my half brother, Nick. Our first home was a little house near Broadway and University Avenues in an area most locals identify with Sheridan Elementary School and a McDonald's.

My mom was the cab driver. She had hustle and street smarts, and she eventually worked her way up to communications director before Uber disrupted the industry. My dad was a technician who could strip any machine down to its component pieces and reassemble it from memory. He also had an artistic side and played guitar in several bands.

I remember hearing stories about crime in the alleys and streets of my first neighborhood in Minneapolis, which is probably why we moved. After a short stint in Brooklyn Park, we settled in the near-north suburb of Columbia Heights. This is when my memories really kick in. We lived just south of a major highway in a modest two-story — not new construction, built in the 1950s. The stairs were in the dead center of the house, and the second-floor attic had been converted to bedrooms, including mine.

If my childhood had a "storybook" phase, this was it, and it didn't last long. I was living in a single-family home and attending a decent elementary school. My parents had worked their way up a bit in their jobs. As far as I knew, everything was great.

It wasn't.

There's no such thing as a "good alcoholic," but my dad was on the severe end of the spectrum. He wasn't the type who went out socially, had some beers and came home. He drank bottles and bottles of hard alcohol. He held his job, but he could get pretty rough and was always on the edge of not being functional. He never physically abused me, my mom or my siblings, but he was aggressive in many other ways.

Some people are "fun drunks" or "lovable drunks." Alcohol brought out my dad's anger. He'd stumble around at night, yelling and arguing with anyone who ticked him off. Everyone ticked him off. If I did something he didn't like, he'd make me stand in the corner for long periods of time.

When he was relatively sober, my dad and I actually spent a decent amount of time together. Minnehaha Falls was his favorite spot (it's still the most photographed site in Minnesota), so we'd go there and explore the area along the Mississippi River. Dad was an outdoorsy type and a National Guardsman — more of a survivalist than a hunter. I can still taste the crackers and peanut butter from the MREs (meals ready to eat) he'd bring on our hikes.

My dad's dad was another key figure in my early childhood. Grandpa Jerry had spent his career salting and sanding roads for the City of Minneapolis. His team would manually shovel salt and sand onto the roads, which is why he had back issues and suffered severe pain for most of his adult life. He'd had his own issues with alcohol in the past, but he was sober by the time I came along. I never saw him take a drink, and I could tell he didn't approve of my dad's lifestyle.

Grandpa Jerry and I also spent time outdoors, mostly fishing and hunting. Hunting with Grandpa Jerry wasn't the typical ritual of tracking deer in the woods. He'd take me on "road trips" in his beat-up station wagon. We couldn't afford to go on private land, so we'd work the ditches or public land. On a typical day, we'd drive around looking for grouse eating pebbles on gravel roads, which they do to help digest food. Grandpa would say, "Let's walk that ditch and see if we can kick that bird up."

Trying to kick up a ring-necked pheasant that can run faster than you on a gravel road … now *that's* old-school hunting.

I rarely spent time with my dad and Grandpa Jerry together, and I never knew why. My grandfather never pulled me aside and said, "Your father has a drinking problem, and here's what that means." But he knew it, and I'm sure it broke his heart. My grandparents loved my dad. He was their golden child. They wanted him to succeed. They always tried to help him. But he kept falling down, literally and figuratively. The man who could repair anything had something inside himself that couldn't be fixed.

My dad's parents were legally married, but separated. Grandma worked a successful job at a major retailer in downtown Minneapolis, and she could be intense and intimidating. My normally confident grandfather would grow timid around her. He'd go to her house every day to do maintenance

Want to live a more Arms Out life? You're not alone! Use the QR code below to register for our FREE newsletter. It's a great way to take your inspiration to the next level.

and grab some food, but every visit felt awkward. I wonder if she kicked him out in his own drinking days and refused to welcome him back after he got sober. I also can't help but wonder about the effect my grandpa's alcoholism and his relationship with my grandma had on my dad. Both of their personalities were passed on to him.

My grandfather never pulled me aside and said, "Your father has a drinking problem, and here's what that means." But he knew it, and I'm sure it broke his heart.

I spent a lot of time in those Columbia Heights days on my own in the backyard. By today's standards, I practically lived outside. Was it an escape? Maybe. I don't remember thinking, "Man, I've got to get out of here." But anytime your parents fight, which mine often did, you tend to remove yourself from the situation.

My toy of choice was a Super Ball. If you're too young to remember, Super Balls were crazy bouncy balls made by Wham-O. Everybody had one. They were so popular that the Super Bowl was named after them. They bounced forever in unpredictable ways, and most kids did tricks with theirs. I had a different game. I'd put on my baseball glove, throw my Super Ball at our back steps, and try to snare it before it got past me.

I could have played my game with a tennis ball, but a Super Ball made it more difficult. I loved not knowing which way it was going to bounce, and the hand-eye coordination I was developing would soon pay dividends. I was subconsciously preparing myself for the unpredictable bounces of life, and one of those was heading right for me.

Core Value: Learning

It might not sound like much, but throwing a Super Ball against the steps was the first memory I have of doing something over and over again to get better at it. Maybe I was trying to escape my dad's alcoholism or my parents' stormy relationship. Whatever the motivation, I wasn't just playing; I was trying to master something.

What are your deepest memories of childhood?
Would you say your family environment was
healthy and positive, or not so much?

Was there an activity you felt so passionate about
that you were obsessed with getting better at it?

Do you have that same drive today?

2. Conflicts Without Resolution

THE "GOOD OLD DAYS" in our Columbia Heights home didn't last long. My dad's drinking gutted the foundation of my parents' marriage, and the walls closed in one day in the early spring of 1990.

My parents invited me, Jamie and Kory down into the living room for a sit-down meeting. I don't remember exactly what they said, but I remember the mood being somber and civil. Our parents didn't say they hated each other. I don't remember anyone yelling or crying. I just remember feeling sad.

Parental separations are always hard to digest, but the part that really hurt was hearing that we could no longer afford our house. I had finally found my neighborhood, my school, my friends, my home. I thought I had found the place where

I was going to grow up. Now I would have to move and start over. Again.

I was close to my mom but felt more emotionally attached to my dad, so I wanted to go wherever he ended up. I was still naïve to how severe his drinking problem was, and I didn't yet grasp that he wasn't capable of taking care of any of us. In reality, following him wasn't an option. We all went with my mother.

Parental separations are always hard to digest, but the part that really hurt was hearing that we could no longer afford our house.

We moved in with my maternal grandparents in Southeast Minneapolis. Today, this trendy neighborhood is lined with expensive apartment complexes with names like "NordHâus." Back then, it was a working-class, Eastern European immigrant community. The only remnant of those days is the famous Kramarczuk's Sausage Company on East Hennepin Avenue.

If my grandparents' property had existed in Chicago, it would have been called a "classic Chicago three-flat." The front door on the left led to a main-level space. The door on the right led to an upper-level space. And a door in the back led to a small studio. The property was close to the University of Minnesota, so my grandparents rented the main level and studio to students and lived in the upper one. After the separation, we moved into the main level.

As luck would have it, a new school opened just three blocks from us. Today, it's called Marcy Arts Magnet Elementary School. When it opened, it was a new concept in education called Marcy Open School. As the "Open" part of the name suggests, it offered a more flexible style of learning, similar to Montessori. Whatever it was, I liked it. I also loved that I could walk there every day, sometimes taking a shortcut through our neighbors' backyards.

This environment might sound peaceful and ideal, but Marcy was still an inner-city school. There was an established pecking order among the kids, and life was punctuated by alpha male showdowns. As the new kid, I got into plenty of fights. In hindsight, I realize that these brawls were an outlet for angry boys from broken homes. I didn't instigate any fights, and I never thought of myself as an angry kid, but I was also from a broken home, and my dad was an addict.

My worst fight serves as a case study in how parenting has changed since my childhood. The St. Anthony Main neighborhood sits where the Mississippi River separates downtown Minneapolis from Southeast and Northeast Minneapolis. In the early '90s, this was the place to be. My friends and I would go there to bike, wander inside the buildings and generally cause trouble.

One day, my Marcy School class went to this area on a field trip, and I started arguing with a classmate who was one of the more authoritative kids at the school. I don't remember what sparked our fight; I just remember needing to stand up for myself. We swung at each other for what felt like hours.

Eventually he pushed me against the brick wall of a pavilion. My head cracked open so badly I needed stitches.

When I got home from the hospital, I stumbled up to my grandparents' place and sprawled out on their couch. Rather than being outraged at my attacker or sympathetic to my injuries, their attitude was "when are you going to learn?" My mom also took my beating in stride. She understood my competitive streak and knew that I was trying to hold my own against an older and bigger opponent, so there was no scolding. Deep down, I think she appreciated the fact that I didn't back down, no matter how much of an underdog I was.

This fight would thicken my skin for hundreds of Goliaths, bullies and online trolls to come. Luckily, a different and more positive experience was also just around the corner.

Core Value: Tenacity

It's not lost on me that I went from hearing my parents fight to getting into a few fights myself. I don't encourage anyone to do that, but my experiences with it do speak to the value of fearlessness. So many people have regrets later in life because they were too intimidated to face a person or obstacle in their youth. I went up against a kid who had more stature (and size) than I did, and I got my head cracked open. But I don't remember him ever bothering me again.

Do you have any regrets over not doing something because it was "too intimidating"?

What's your first memory of feeling fearless or tenacious?

What are you most afraid to do in your life or career right now?

Uncle Eric

My Uncle Eric was one of my biggest influences growing up. Though he was born with Down syndrome, my mom's parents insisted that he not be treated differently than anybody else. They even took the (then) unusual step of integrating him into "regular" high school, and though I can't prove it for sure, I think their approach made a huge impact on his life. And mine.

Eric accomplished so much in his life. He participated in the first study of early infant stimulation through the University of Minnesota. He graduated from Roosevelt High School in Minneapolis and attended his senior prom. He was a Special Olympics standout, and he was the first person in the state to letter in high school for his participation in the Special Olympics.

I also loved seeing Eric perform with the Interact Center for the Visual and Performing Arts, an organization for artists with disabilities. Eric was Interact's founding actor when they started in 1996, and he performed with them for over 20 years. Most notably, he toured the U.S. and the world playing the title role in a play called "Bubba Nielsen: Endangered Species."

Everyone loved Eric, and we were all impressed by how much he accomplished in his life (he died in 2013). But what I remember most is the simple act of watching professional wrestling with him. Eric *loved* wrestling. He knew every wrestler's name and history, and he had dozens of VHS tapes featuring all the different stars. We would spend hours together, just hanging out and watching all of it, over and over again.

As my grandparents wished, I never treated Eric differently from other people. And by doing that, I learned so much from him. People who grow up around Down syndrome often gain a different perspective on life — a greater appreciation for opportunities, and a higher level of patience, kindness and, most importantly, empathy.

ARMS
OUT

3. Don't Stop Until You Hear the Whistle

I'VE ALWAYS BEEN obsessed with sports. I'm not exaggerating when I say that I pitched nearly every game for my Little League baseball teams (I have the elbow problems to prove it), but my early wrestling days in fourth grade would deliver my first big life lessons.

Despite having never wrestled before, I won most of my matches and eventually qualified for the nationals for my age and weight class. I succeeded because I developed The Move. When I learned that you weren't allowed to get your opponent into a headlock unless you also had one of their arms, I figured out how to take advantage of that rule. As soon as the ref blew his whistle to start a match, I would grab my opponent's right arm with my left hand, yank it in, get them in a headlock, flip them over and throw them down. Boom! Match over.

The boys I competed against looked like they'd been wrestling from the day they were born, and The Move worked as long as I surprised them with it at the start of the match. If I didn't, I was in serious trouble. Unfortunately, by the time I reached the nationals competition in Fargo, North Dakota, some of the other wrestlers had figured out how to defend The Move. I placed third, but I felt disappointed. More importantly, I realized that I didn't love wrestling, probably because it wasn't enough of a team sport.

When I moved to Southeast Minneapolis with my mom and siblings, I shifted my attention to basketball. In the summer before starting sixth grade, I experienced the most important sports moment of my life, and that Super Ball might have had something to do with it.

That summer, I played hours of pickup basketball outside my elementary school. I had never played before, and I didn't have any training or coaching. YouTube didn't exist, so I couldn't pull up videos showing me how to dribble or shoot. But I could feel myself getting the hang of it fast. Something about basketball came naturally to me.

"You're going to try out for a basketball team," my mom announced one day after returning from work. Maybe she had noticed my progress, or maybe she just wanted me out of her hair during the summer. The team she had in mind was called Minneapolis South Traveling. Today, it would be part of the Amateur Athletic Union system. Back then, it consisted of eight or nine of the best sixth-grade players from each Minneapolis neighborhood — an all-star team of 11- and 12-

year-old boys.

I was all in.

I remember every detail of that tryout like it was yesterday. My mom packed me into her Crown Victoria sedan (cabbies bought these cars at police auctions for their personal use). She dropped me off at a place in Minneapolis called Powderhorn Park, and I stepped into my first elite sports environment. Most of the boys were already well known in basketball circles at that level. People don't believe me when I tell them that one kid was already 6 feet, 6 inches tall and could reverse dunk, but I can still see it in my head.

Despite the talent around me, I wasn't intimidated. I treated that tryout like my life depended on making the team, and something magical happened. I found myself dribbling, shooting and scoring like never before — against people twice my size. Playing at that level in a pickup game was one thing. Doing it in an organized gym was another. I felt energized, almost invincible, and I wanted the feeling to last forever.

"How did it go?" my mom asked when she picked me up in the Crown Victoria three hours later.

"Pretty well," I said, underplaying it.

A day later, we got the call that I had made the team. I was over the moon. I don't think I was actually good enough to be on that team, but I'm guessing the coaches liked my spirit and saw my potential.

I ended up being the sixth man, right on the edge of being a starter, and the experience changed my life. Our team obliterated the competition. Our style was "no quit, no mercy." We were aggressive and relentless. We pressed the entire game, our tall center blocking every shot and inbound pass.

Today, the parents of kids on those other teams would accuse us of being unsportsmanlike. Back then, you kept going no matter what. Years later, when I saw the documentary series on the USA Dream Team, I identified with their mentality. On any scale, when you put talented and driven players together, something happens. You mess around in practice, then the energy ramps up during scrimmages. Someone sets an aggressive pick or throws an elbow. Tempers flare, fights break out. Eventually, you come back together as a team, take that intensity into your games and run over your competition.

The coaches were passionate about basketball, but they were also generous men who worked hard to help underprivileged city kids build confidence, gain leadership skills, and grow as players and people.

That Minneapolis South Traveling team did indeed travel. We took buses all over Minnesota and to nearby states, and we rarely lost. I fell in love with winning at a high level. It taught me to believe in myself, believe in my team and not even *think* about stopping until you hear the whistle blow.

I also couldn't help but notice how the entire operation was run, especially the people involved. The coaches were passionate about basketball, but they were also generous men who worked hard to help underprivileged city kids build confidence, gain leadership skills, and grow as players and people.

Those coaches prepared me to deal with challenging situations to come. But nothing could have prepared me for what was about to happen outside a Minneapolis grocery store.

Core Values: Tenacity, Learning, Generosity

I was more tenacious about basketball than anything else in my life. That spirit helped me earn a spot on a high-level team where I raised my game even more. I also learned generosity from the coaches who volunteered their time and truly cared about underprivileged city kids.

What's your first memory of generosity? Was it something a parent did? Another relative, teacher or coach? How did it make you feel?

How are you generous in your current life? Are you as generous as you'd like to be? What's the #1 talent you could share with others to improve their lives?

ARMS
OUT

4. Gun to the Head at the Red Owl

MY SOUTHEAST MINNEAPOLIS years had their ups and downs. On the downside, drinking remained my dad's primary interest. My brother and sister still visited him on weekends, but I was out of the picture by choice.

On the upside, my mom's taxi company promoted her to communications director, a position where she managed all the dispatchers. It's hard to explain this job to younger people today. Mom basically oversaw a bunch of land-based air traffic controllers who connected cab drivers to customers in the pre-internet world. Drivers would check in at different points ("Hey, I'm at the mall"), and the dispatchers would manually assign them to passengers based on their proximity to each other.

On the relationship front, I noticed a new set of characters hanging out with my mom — men who didn't have many resources and were always hustling to make ends meet. Eventually, my mom got pregnant by one of these new characters: a guy we'll call Paul.

Paul was also in the taxi business, and he was rough. Really rough. He once tried to win me over by giving me a Haro bike, which seemed like a generous gesture until I noticed that the serial number had been scratched off. My mom has now been with her partner, Skip, for over 20 years, but back then she tended to date "works in progress." She thought she could fix these men, and Paul was no exception.

Mom ended her relationship with Paul when she realized that he wasn't the best influence on her kids. After he disappeared, a new boyfriend entered the picture. "Brian" was also in the taxi business. He struck me as an aggressive character — and I was exhausted from being around so many men who made poor decisions — but I wanted to give him a chance. Unfortunately, we butted heads as soon as he moved in with us. We could co-exist, but I knew we would never be close.

One fall night while my mom was still at work, I told Brian that I needed some cereal. I was hungry all the time from playing sports, and I needed my Wheaties.

People from Minneapolis might remember the Red Owl grocery store that sat on the corner of Central and Hennepin, diagonally from the Aveda headquarters. Brian and I went there to get my Wheaties and some other items, and as we walked back out onto the street, a man stepped in front of us and blocked our path. It was Paul.

I don't know if Paul's arrival was a coincidence or a plan, but seeing Brian threw him into a jealous rage. He was clearly in a state of blackout adrenaline — maybe drunk or on drugs — and he looked like a completely different person.

"I'm gonna kill you right now!" he screamed at Brian, pinning him against the hood of a car. Then he whipped out a gun and pressed it to Brian's head.

The customers inside the Red Owl watched from their checkout lanes, frozen. "This isn't a good idea!" I heard someone shout. "There's a better way to resolve this!" The "someone" was me. Helpless to do anything physically, words started pouring out of my mouth.

"You don't want to do this!" I shouted. "Let's figure out a different way!"

As Paul pushed the gun harder into Brian's temple, I kept trying to reason with him. I don't know if I talked for 10 minutes or 10 seconds, but something finally worked. Paul put his gun away and slapped Brian hard across the face.

"You're f***in' lucky Kris is here right now!" he said, and he walked away.

When Brian and I crawled back into his car, I sensed that we weren't going to talk about what just happened. He was in face-saving mode. He wanted to show me that he was still tough, as if maintaining his masculinity was more important than the fact that he had nearly gotten his brains blown out in front of his girlfriend's son.

Brian told my mom what happened, and she was horrified. Then Paul started calling her. When she refused to answer, he started calling my grandparents. When they stonewalled him, he left messages shouting things like, "I'm gonna burn your whole f***in' house down!"

Paul was angry and armed. He also knew where our family lived. Within a week, we were on the run — as in "pack your bags we're leaving in an hour" on the run. Soon our entire family, including Brian and Nick, was speeding north in Brian's car. I knew what we were escaping from. I had no idea what we were heading into.

Core Value: Empathy

Trying to save someone who has a gun to their head isn't the ideal way to learn empathy. Then again, it's hard to watch something like that without imagining the gun pointed at *your* head. Despite my issues with Brian, I didn't want any harm to come to him. And who knows, maybe Paul put his gun away because he felt a tiny drop of empathy for me as I pleaded for him to stop.

What brought out your empathy as a child? People in need? A neighbor? Animals? A friend who was less fortunate?

How do you express empathy on a professional level? Do you empathize as much as you should with your colleagues and customers?

41

Fishing

Despite my urban upbringing, a painting of my youth might show a boy rowing across a remote lake by himself.

Fishing has been a key throughline in my life. When I was a kid, we'd drive up to my grandparents' cabin in Grantsburg, Wisconsin, on summer weekends. While everyone else watched game shows and drank cocktails, I'd climb into their leaky johnboat and paddle out onto Spirit Lake by myself.

With limited resources, I had to be creative. The anchor string was too short for deep water, so I'd hit some shallow hot spots and fish for bass using my $19 Zebco combo special. For bait, I'd use a few plastic frogs and some nightcrawlers I'd harvest myself by flooding our backyard.

These trips gave me an outlet of solitude. Today, fishing is more of a social activity. A key moment came when I sold the house of well-known outdoorsman Tony Capra. We realized that we share the entrepreneurial bug, and now we fish all the time on his state-of-the-art boat (the screens alone probably cost more than my grandparents' cabin). The equipment may have changed, but the passion is the same.

One of my favorite fishing stories shows how much I love spontaneity. In January 2019, I was on a guided adventure off the coast of Tamarindo in Costa Rica. As I was fishing for marlin, sailfish and tuna with my partner,

Gina, and some friends, our guide mentioned that he was supposed to leave for the Pelagic Rockstar fishing tournament in Quepos, but his team had backed out at the last minute.

"Let's go!" I said. (Those words again.)

The Pelagic Rockstar Offshore Tournament is considered the largest fishing competition in Central America, with competitors catching and releasing over 1,000 billfish and earning over $1 million in prize money. It was above my skill level, but as you're about to see in this book, I love putting myself in positions where I have to learn fast and raise my own bar.

I drove eight hours across Costa Rica to get to Quepos in time for the tournament, and my friend Luke flew down to meet me. We didn't win any money, but I didn't care. Anyone who fishes knows that it's really about reeling in great stories.

ARMS
OUT

5. Chain Saws, Pellet Guns & a Key Life Decision

PEQUOT LAKES IS less than a three-hour drive from Minneapolis, but it might as well be on another planet. When my family arrived there after fleeing the Twin Cities, the town's population was under 1,000. We weren't even in the town; we were outside of it, hidden among the birch and Norway pines. We were completely isolated from the world in the dead of a cold, dark Minnesota winter.

Before we left, I was told that Brian owned "a house and some land up north." Upon arrival, I realized that the word "house" was an exaggeration. The small, ramshackle cabin I was about to enter — which six people were now supposed to live in — was a half-finished, slapdash collection of DIY construction done in spurts, with no indoor plumbing and a wood stove for heat.

I felt like I had traveled back in time a hundred years. Overnight, I had gone from a city kid with tons of friends, who spent every second of his spare time playing sports, to being a stranger, lost and alone in the woods with my immediate family and a man I didn't get along with. I also learned that instead of walking to my familiar school through neighbors' backyards, I would have to sit on a bus for three hours a day going to and from a new school where I didn't know a soul.

That wasn't even the worst part.

Norway red pines can grow up to 150 feet, and their dense trunks can stretch 5 feet in diameter. These trees would soon become my worst enemies. As other kids slept or watched Saturday cartoons, I would be forced awake at 5:30 a.m., including on school days. Brian would tell me to bundle up in multiple layers, then put me behind the wheel of a huge Massey-Harris tractor.

Going through the woods brought back memories of kicking up the ruffed grouse with my grandfather when I was a kid. But this wasn't nearly as adventurous. I wasn't going to be hunting, and I wasn't going to be hiking and building forts in our new forest home. I was there to chop down trees. Lots of trees.

My typical routine went as follows:

- Drive the tractor through deep snow to a Norway pine.

- Cut it with a massive chain saw, alternating sides.

- Make sure the last cut is on the opposite side that the tree is going to fall on (otherwise, my saw might get stuck and I'd get crushed).

- Attach a huge chain to the fallen tree.

- Drag it to an accessible area.

- Saw it into 12-foot sections.

- Wait for someone from the local sawmill to pick it up.

No physical labor I experience will ever compare to those dark mornings, sometimes in 20-below weather. The forest would be eerily quiet except for the sounds of the occasional ruffed grouse or white-tailed deer. At the age of 12, I would work a massive chain saw, and it would kick back whenever it hit a knot in the wood. Unfortunately, Norway pines have lots of knots. One morning, dead from exhaustion as I was cutting a tree down to the right length, my saw kicked back and ripped my snowpants. I looked down expecting to see blood and a half-amputated limb, but somehow the blades avoided cutting off my leg. I respected that huge chain saw after that, and I worked twice as hard to stay alert no matter how tired I felt.

In addition to selling the wood, we used some of it to heat the cabin. Temperature control was a challenge with our woodstove, so rooms were either so cold that you could see your breath, or so sauna-like that your clothes would stick to your skin. There was no in-between.

Despite the hardships, Pequot Lakes did offer a preview of my entrepreneurial side. I wanted a pellet gun worse than the kid in "A Christmas Story" wanted a Red Ryder Air Rifle. I decided to buy one by selling some of my old video games to a pawnshop I had spotted in nearby Brainerd. When I arrived with an armful of games, the guy behind the counter had no idea what he was about to get into.

"You said you'd give me $10 for three games, but now you're only offering me $12 for four?" I said. "How does that make any sense?" I was a natural haggler. I'm not sure whether my bravado annoyed or entertained the pawnshop guy, but it worked. We came to an agreement. I took my aggressively negotiated money to purchase my new pellet gun. When we got home, I proudly took it into the forest and did what boys do with pellet guns … until I quickly ran out of CO_2 cartridges. Oops.

Speaking of guns, Brian started carrying a real one after his run-in with Paul. I think he also wore it to intimidate me, but that didn't stop me from laying into him whenever I could, which was often. As the Minnesota winter dragged on, our relationship further deteriorated. I was working my tail off to keep the place going, and we were still barely getting by — sometimes reduced to getting free groceries at a food bank and relying on donated gifts for the holidays.

"This place sucks!" I screamed at Brian one day. "This house isn't even ready for us to live in!" I called my grandpa and pleaded with him to rescue me as tears ran down my face. "Get me out of here! Take me anywhere but here!" I screamed at him. Hearing these words from his grandson must have broken my grandfather's heart, but he chose to stay out of the conflict.

Spring's arrival didn't thaw the tensions between Brian and me. Eventually, my mom lost patience too. I don't remember what led up to it, but one day she put her foot down and said, "Brian, we're going back to where we're from!" Those words were music to my ears. I was ready to leave no matter what. I had already imagined myself hitchhiking back to Minneapolis, or even walking the 150 miles myself. I didn't care how long it would take or if I had a place to sleep when I got there. I had one thought, and it has stayed with me for the rest of my life: *The only way you're going to make a better life for yourself is by taking charge. It's 100% up to you.*

Lots of people reach crossroads like these, especially when they grow up in challenging circumstances. Sometimes it's a breaking point that causes you to give up hope and fall into drug use or other self-destructive behaviors. Other times, it can be a clarifying moment in which you embrace full accountability for your life and decide that you're going to fight through every obstacle.

I had one thought, and it has stayed with me for the rest of my life: The only way you're going to make a better life for yourself is by taking charge. It's 100% up to you.

Luckily, I chose the second path. After my seventh-grade year, we headed back south to the Twin Cities. I didn't know where I was going to live, which school I would be attending or who my next set of friends were going to be, but I felt an inner calm. No one saw it on the outside, but I knew it on the inside: I was a different person. I had always had an inner drive. Now I'd found a new gear. Look out.

Core Value: Owning It

My exile in the Minnesota woods pushed me to fully embrace accountability. I felt like I had no control over my life, so I decided to change that forever. It's no surprise that I became an entrepreneur!

Have you had a moment (or moments) in your life where you've fully taken responsibility for your actions, or do you tend to blame others?

Have you seen people go down a path of self-destruction in part because they refused to take ownership of their lives?

ARMS OUT

6. Fridley, Football & Finding My Footing

AFTER OUR EXILE in the woods, we moved back to my grandparents' house. With resources tight and jobs scarce, my mom looked outside the city for an affordable new place of our own, and she eventually received approval for a fourplex apartment in Fridley, 10 miles north of Minneapolis.

I was overjoyed to move into a modern building that looked nothing like Brian's slipshod cabin. But when the bus came to take me to yet another new school, a familiar shame washed over me. While my classmates lived in single-family homes, I lived in a government-subsidized apartment. A psychiatrist could probably draw a line from these feelings of embarrassment to me eventually wanting to help people find their dream homes. It's no accident that I've frequently rented single- and multi-family properties I've owned to people in situations like the ones I faced growing up.

The school year also brought back another familiar feeling: whiplash. I was dizzy from all the moving. But once again, my mom (and sports) came to the rescue. I had never played football, and I wasn't sure I wanted to start now. But when Mom signed me up for a team, a familiar voice inside my head said "just do it" long before Nike made that their slogan.

Fridley had lightweight, heavyweight and combination football teams for eighth graders. I was slightly over lightweight, and I was put with the heavyweights. That's when I met a man who would become one of the most important figures in my life: John Swanson.

Coach Swanson was the type of leader who pushes his kids hard — not because he's mean, but because he wants to raise the bar and inspire them to be their best. He was disciplined, assertive, competitive and caring. For a kid like me, that was the ideal combination.

At first, Coach Swanson put me at nose tackle. That's the easiest position to play when you don't know much about football. Problem is, you get beat up. And the bigger, more experienced offensive players absolutely crushed me. Remember those scenes in "Rudy" when he's put on Notre Dame's practice squad and gets plowed into the dirt by linemen twice his size? That was me.

I was physical and athletic, but I didn't know where to go or what to do. I also didn't know the pulling techniques, so I constantly got outmaneuvered and blown off the ball. Compared to basketball, my early football experience was *not* fun. But any thoughts I might have had about quitting were erased when Coach Swanson took me aside one day and said, "Look, Kris, you're a good athlete. Stick with it, and you're going to be a *really* good football player."

Swanson's confidence in me was critical at that age. I needed someone who was hard on me but also believed in me. He gave me the courage I needed to believe in myself and be patient. Behind the scenes, he also showed incredible generosity. Knowing that my mom couldn't afford some of the bigger, more expensive equipment I needed, he made sure I got it anyway.

I learned a lot more than football that year, and I started a friendship with John Swanson that has continued across countless golf outings and sporting events to this day.

Swanson's confidence in me was critical at that age. I needed someone who was hard on me but also believed in me. He gave me the courage I needed to believe in myself and be patient.

Unfortunately, I also still had a knack for getting into fights, and they ramped up dramatically in my last year of middle school. Most were with a kid I'll call Trevor. He and I fought weekly in the locker room. I don't mean a shove here or a slap there. I'm talking full-blown, don't-stop-until-you're-completely-gassed swinging. Fights among my football teammates were like a sport within a sport: Instead of breaking them up, my teammates would watch and cheer.

More skin-thickening for me.

Life did improve that year. I matured. I made some new friends. A few girls took an interest in me, which helped my confidence. This feeling continued into Fridley High School — as did Swanson's influence, because he coached our ninth-grade basketball team.

By this point in my childhood, I lived and breathed sports. My point-guard skills continued to improve, and I thrived in football. I moved to tight end and started scoring touchdowns. Then I moved to wide receiver and scored even more. By 10th grade, I was throwing my hand in the air like Randy Moss, and my friend (and starting quarterback) Nick Arellano was hitting me all over the field.

In hindsight, sports probably saved my life during this period. Basketball and football gave me something to focus on and look forward to. They became my entire reason for being. From the moment I woke up, I just wanted to make it to 3:00 so I could play more sports.

Later in life, you realize the superficiality of trophies. But with all the negative things swirling around me at that time, athletic achievement gave my life meaning. *Things are bad at home, but over here I'm winning.* It was as simple as that.

Winning is a drug. When my summer traveling basketball team won game after game, I remember thinking, *Wow, this is how life can feel.* But if we had lost every game, would I have lost my confidence as well? Would I have quit sports and gone into a shell? It's a "nature vs. nurture" question, and it's probably a little of both. On the court, I became an obsessive maniac who had to win at all costs. As I get older, I've learned that pathological competitiveness isn't always healthy. At some point, you have to channel your intensity into helping others instead of defeating them.

Today, my field of play is the stage. Whether it's 20 people or 20,000, I get a rush from speaking and motivating. I've also had to work hard to feel comfortable in front of crowds. I used to rely on PowerPoint presentations and repeat the information on each slide. Today, I can speak on a topic for four hours

Want to live a more Arms Out life? You're not alone! Use the QR code below to register for our FREE newsletter. It's a great way to take your inspiration to the next level.

off the cuff without a break. In fact, the longer I go, the more energized I get. I have to be dragged off the stage.

Looking back on my high school sports years, I realize that I was a bit imbalanced. But sports set me on the right path. Mostly, they taught me the importance of showing up. I showed up to wrestle when I didn't know anything about wrestling. I showed up to that basketball tryout in sixth grade and earned a spot on a team I wasn't expected to make. And I kept showing up in the early days of football, even when I was getting my butt kicked.

Showing up continues to be an important theme in my life. No matter how hard things get, I refuse to run away or disappear. Am I just stubborn? Maybe. But a voice inside my head always says, *No matter how much abuse you take, keep showing up.*

In high school, that mindset was starting to pay off. With

colleges recruiting me in both football and basketball, I finally started to see a path for myself. The future was positive, and it was all about sports. Unfortunately, my life was about to get turned upside down like never before.

Core Values: Tenacity and Generosity

My tenacity around sports gave me a focus, a source of self-esteem and a positive vision for my future. Key to that was Coach Swanson's generosity in telling me how much he believed in me and the special attention he paid to helping me reach my full potential.

What gives you a boost of self-esteem in your life?

Have you had a teacher or coach who believed in you and helped you live up to your potential?

Do you do that for other people?

7. My Dad's Homicide

AT THIS POINT in my life, my dad lived in a seedy apartment complex just outside of Minneapolis. I avoided seeing him, because things didn't go well when I did. Two particular visits led to a breaking point in our relationship.

During the first of these visits, I played with some sharp metal stars that my dad liked to throw at his walls like darts. I threw one that stuck to a door, and he wasn't happy with that. When I was a little kid, he would punish me by making me stand in a corner for 10 minutes. I was older and stronger now, but that didn't matter to him. He still saw me as a child, so he once again told me to stand in the corner, and this time he planned on keeping me there for hours. No surprise, he was drunk.

"Longer!" he would shout when I would make any kind

of movement. Finally I'd had enough.

"This is why I don't come here!" I screamed at him, and I walked out the door.

The second event happened during the holidays. Dad's drinking had gotten worse, if that was even possible, and I could tell that we were coming to a fork in the road. I had never expected big, lavish gifts from him. But that year, he gave me an oversized coloring book. Something about that moment stood out to me. *You're at a point in your life where all you can give your teenage son for the holidays is a coloring book? This is where things end.*

I was more right than I wanted to be. That March, I got the 911 page from my mom that led to the events I wrote about in the Introduction to this book: My dad's drunken girlfriend had run him over and killed him. There would be no final confrontation, no reconciliation, no goodbye. Dad was gone forever.

Everyone deals with grief and trauma in their own way. The closest I came to therapy was spending a day with my friend Luke. His dad was also an alcoholic, so we related on that level, and one day we went for a drive in the general direction of his parents' cabin in Wisconsin. We stopped to fish at a familiar pond on the way, and we talked. With the exception of spending time with my family during and after the funeral, reeling in those perch and crappies with Luke was the longest I ever took to process my father's death. It sounds very "stoic Minnesotan," but I think it's all I needed at the time.

Unfortunately, Dad's death also created tensions in the

family. As his dependents, my siblings and I were entitled to his possessions and a small payout from his military life insurance policy. But the situation became complicated by the fact that we were under 18 and my dad didn't have a written will. The state assigned us a *guardian ad litem*, and the courts eventually straightened everything out, but the attorney's fees took a big chunk out of what was already a modest amount of money.

The feelings of conflict, lost time and wasted money from this situation would later play a role in me creating the *Guaranteed Cash Offer* program and writing my book *Guaranteed Cash Offer: Sell Your Property Fast with Total Convenience and No Commissions*. So many homes are sold around life-changing events, including job relocations, divorce and deaths in the family. I've seen how a deceased parent's possessions — especially their house — can cause stress among their heirs. I know from personal experience: That's the last thing you want to deal with when you're grieving.

I ran into our *guardian ad litem* 20 years later when he was retired and in his 70s. Someone referred me to him when he wanted to sell his house, and I sold it in a day. We sat at the kitchen table and talked about my dad, and he remembered every detail. I'll never forget how good it felt when he looked at me and said, "Looks like you're doing pretty well for yourself."

Core Values: Empathy, Generosity, Owning It

My father tried and failed to "own" and address his alcoholism, and that played a role in his early death. But despite the tragedy, I learned a lot from the generosity of Luke and others who empathized with our situation and showed their love for us during that time.

Are you (or is someone you love) having trouble addressing addiction issues? No one can do it on their own, and the longer you fail to own the problem, the worse it's going to get.

How do you show empathy and generosity when someone you care about experiences tragedy? As Luke showed me, sometimes the best thing you can do is simply make the time and listen.

The One Time I Quit

After my dad died, the rest of my high school years proved to be less eventful. I played varsity basketball and football. Coach Swanson continued to be the father figure I needed. I got along with my football coach. But my basketball coach and I never saw eye to eye, and that led to a series of events that stay with me to this day.

At the end of my junior-year basketball season, right before the state tournament, I was called into the office by the athletic director and my coach. They told me I smelled like marijuana, which came as a shock to me because I wasn't a drug user. They thought I was high. In no uncertain terms, I assured them that I was not. It was my word against theirs. They had all the power, and they suspended me for the last few basketball games.

Nothing stings like being falsely accused, and I still don't know what prompted that whole situation. All I know is that sometimes coming from the city puts a target on your back, and people assume the worst about you. Whatever the reason, I couldn't get out of the punishment. I didn't have much fight left in me, and I sat out.

Toward the end of my senior year, I reached a breaking point. I was having the game of my life through three quarters, but my coach sat me in the fourth. I couldn't understand why, and I got angry. After the game, I grabbed all my jerseys from my car, marched into the locker room and threw them all on the floor.

"I'm done!" I shouted, then stormed out without turning around.

Coach Swanson called me later that night. "Why didn't you talk to me before you quit?" he said. "I could have gotten this resolved."

"I don't know," I said. "I've just had enough."

I'd never quit anything before, and I still regret that decision. I was more burned out than I would have admitted at the time. I'd been playing football and basketball year-round. Maybe my body was making me take a break. Maybe my spirit was calling in the emotional debts I'd racked up. Or maybe I didn't need sports because I was in a better place emotionally. Was it a huge mistake, or did I stop playing exactly when I needed to? I still don't know.

My decision had deeper ramifications. I'd been laser focused on being recruited for football, and Division II and III schools had expressed interest in me. I even thought I might play at the University of Minnesota. Now I started to lose motivation. From March until the end of August, I wasn't playing sports, doing the same level of workouts or following up on communication from recruiters. They pay attention to things like that, and they lost interest in me when I lost interest in them.

I was still having fun and enjoying life, but I started to wonder if there was more to it than grinding out sports all day.

There was, and I was about to find it in college.

ARMS
OUT

8. Mankato to Mazatlán: A Travel Business Takes Off

BEFORE I TALK about my initiation into the business world, I have to share two high school job experiences that laid the groundwork for exploring my entrepreneurial side in college.

The first was at a fishing pro shop. After weeks of sorting nightcrawlers, minnows and leeches, I was promoted to working the register. One day in winter, a co-worker named Rich came in with a fishbowl of handmade ice-fishing lures that he wanted to sell for $3 each. He wasn't sure if customers would bite, so to speak, and I took his doubt as a challenge.

"Ten bucks says I can sell all your lures today," I said.

Rich thought I was crazy. But hey, easy money for him, right? We shook hands, and I went to work.

My strategy was simple: Everyone who walked into our store needed a fishing license and bait for a nearby ice-fishing tournament, and that gave me my opening.

"Do you have the hot new lure for the fishing tournament?" I asked each customer as they checked out. We'd strike up a conversation. I'd learn about their lives, how long they'd been going to the tournament, their biggest catch and the one that got away, and they'd eventually buy the product. I can't remember if the big prize was a new truck or thousands of dollars, but I'm pretty sure that "hot new lure" won the competition that year.

My colleagues at the pro shop were amazed at my ability to connect with people. Some of them had been working there for years and had never tried to build rapport with customers. I had the advantage of being a "disruptor": I tried something new, and within a few hours, that fishbowl was as empty as Rich's wallet.

Winning that bet felt as good as winning at sports. Before long, the owner put me in charge of selling just about everything in the store. Years later, he hired me to sell the building.

Later, I worked at a sporting goods store inside a mall. That year, the L.A. Lakers released a retro jersey in the style of the old Minneapolis Lakers: baby blue with gold trim and a big "MPLS" across the front. With Kobe and Shaq wearing it, it quickly became the hottest piece of sports equipment in the country. I saw an opportunity.

When the store received a small shipment of the jerseys, I used my employee discount to buy them at $30 each, offered them on eBay and found that people were willing to pay up to $400 for them. I did the same thing with the next shipment and got the same enthusiastic response. Then I borrowed my grandparents' credit card and ordered every jersey in our store's entire network. They sold faster than I could get my hands on them.

"What are you doing with all these jerseys?" my manager asked me one day. I sheepishly answered that I had a little side business on eBay. Three weeks later, some regional-level people swooped in. Long story short, that was my last day at the store.

That experience showed a pattern I would repeat often: seeing an opportunity — some might say a loophole — and driving a truck through it. It also taught me the Kenny Rogers Rule: "You've got to know when to hold 'em and know when to fold 'em." By the time I received my last batch of jerseys, Nike's production had more than caught up. Supply far exceeded demand, and the jerseys eventually went the way of Beanie Babies and Big Mouth Billy Bass.

That experience showed a pattern I would repeat often: seeing an opportunity — some might say a loophole — and driving a truck through it.

Despite my early success in business, I enrolled at Minnesota State University, Mankato in 2000 to become a teacher. Officially, I was an education major. Unofficially, I was about to earn my degree in entrepreneurship.

House parties were my introductory class. I lived on the seventh floor of a huge dorm my freshman year. Older friends of mine lived in off-campus houses, and their parties were so huge that they would sell tickets to finance their massive keg investments. In short order, I became known as "the guy who can bring the dorm crowd to house parties." I sold massive numbers of house-party tickets and used my small commission to help pay bills and tuition. It was fun, but my next venture was about to take me a lot farther, literally.

As a kid, the only trip I can remember was taking a Greyhound bus to Fort Sill, Oklahoma, when my dad was in basic training. In college, the travel bug bit hard. I took road trips to nearby campuses. And because I'm a city kid at heart, I also loved going back to Minneapolis to visit my friend Steve at the University of Minnesota. On one of these visits, a chance meeting sent my life south in a good way.

One day when I was hanging out at Steve's off-campus house, he introduced me to his new friend Ryan. Ryan was my opposite: a small-town kid who was now living in the city and loving his freedom. In the course of our conversation, Ryan told me that he had recently met the owner of a vacation company who wanted him to run his spring break travel business. Ryan said yes, but he didn't seem nearly as excited about it as I was.

"Wait, you have the company card to a business that sells spring break packages to Mazatlán?" I said. "You're talking about flying to Mexico and staying there for a month every year? Let's go!"

I was like a puppy who'd found a new toy. Ryan probably thought I was a little weird, but my enthusiasm won him over, and we soon started working together.

The company chartered flights through Champion Air, Ryanair and other discount airlines, then packaged them with hotel rooms and sold them to college students. I'd never been to Mexico, but before I knew it, I was leading groups of students down to Mazatlán and creating wildly popular offers despite having never taken a marketing class.

All four years at Mankato, I sold a crazy number of trips. Every spring break, I'd fly down to Mexico for spring break (and sometimes longer, but I always managed to keep up with my schoolwork). By the second year of our operation, I had acquired a deep understanding of the business model. I couldn't stop new ideas from popping into my head. And one day, I got a big one.

I noticed that once students arrived in Mazatlán, they would buy a party package from our much bigger competitor. For a flat fee, they'd receive a red wristband that allowed them to drink for free at all the bars. The company sold tons of these wristbands, and their party packages brought in most of their profits. They had a foolproof system in every way. Except one.

"What if we developed our own party packages, but we sold them to students *before* they boarded the planes?" I said to Ryan.

I took on the challenge of selling a seven-day party

package for $79–$99 in airports around the country. We're talking 2001, so no Orbitz, Travelocity or Priceline. You couldn't even book a flight online. I manually printed out flight schedules and laid them out on the floor. Then I put together a schedule, sent our reps to the airports armed with backpacks of party package tickets and our *blue* wristbands, and prayed.

The moment of truth arrived that spring in Mazatlán. I stood inside the airport on one side of the gate. The competitors' reps stood on the other side, armed with their red wrist bands. When the first group of passengers stepped into the gate, the reps' jaws hit the floor. Every student was wearing a royal blue wristband. We had already sold them their party packages. They didn't need the competitor anymore.

Every plane brought another wave of blue wristbands, and the competing reps were *not* happy. This college punk had just disrupted their entire business model, and eventually they had no choice but to give away their party packages for free to save face. I didn't feel guilty. It was a classic case of a more nimble David outmaneuvering a slower Goliath. The Goliath had stopped innovating, safe in the belief that whatever worked yesterday would work again today. That's not how it works. Ever.

Ryan and I didn't stop there, either. Our next move was to hit the road in a Travelmaster RV to sell more trips. The RV was owned by our friend Willy's brother, and Willy came along as the driver. We would contact popular local bars in college towns and say, "We're giving away a spring break trip. If you promote it, we'll do it at your bar and bring in tons of people!" Huge crowds would show up and sign up. We'd announce a winner, then we'd send everyone else a "you didn't win this time, but here's something else for you" message. We would give people value in the form of a gift or offer, then continue to prospect them for paid trips.

The Goliath had stopped innovating, safe in the belief that whatever worked yesterday would work again today. That's not how it works. Ever.

Every promotion I came up with worked better than expected. Because I ran the logistics, I learned the details that go into making an offer work. But despite the success, I never thought, *Maybe I should be in business or marketing.* The closest thing to an entrepreneur in my family was Grandma Phyllis, who had started a small business around packaging local business coupons for new arrivals to the neighborhood. She only spent a few hours a day on it, but it was successful enough that a huge grocery chain nearly bought it before they decided to start their own instead.

Was I born with the entrepreneur gene, or did circumstances push me in that direction? It's another "nature vs. nurture" question, and I'll share more thoughts on that topic later. For now, I was going wherever my passions took me. That approach was paying my college tuition, and it was also about to land me in a different kind of leadership position.

Core Values: Learning, Tenacity

My early entrepreneurial adventures taught me how to be a quick starter and learn on the job. With the travel business, I taught myself the entire model, then found a way to disrupt it. I also used my tenacity to keep stealing market share from the Goliath. Their biggest weakness? Being a top dog that refused to learn new tricks.

Are you the type of person who can't experience anything — a restaurant, a grocery store, an entertainment complex — without thinking about how it could be done better?

In what situations do you find yourself learning without even realizing you're doing it?

The Art of the Pivot

In the winter of 2003, the state of Minnesota (a.k.a. the State of Hockey) was in a frenzy. In only their third season in the NHL, the Minnesota Wild had advanced to the third round of the Stanley Cup Playoffs after surviving two 3–1 deficits. Now they were facing Vancouver with a chance to play in the finals for the first time since the Minnesota North Stars got there in 1991.

My friend Tony and I were huge Wild fans, and we were also passionate entrepreneurs, so we hatched a plan (Tony would say I talked him into it): We bought two prime tickets on the glass for a Wild–Canucks game at Xcel Center in St. Paul for about $400 each with the intention of selling them outside the arena for a handsome profit.

There was only one problem: This was way before things like Venmo and StubHub, and as we soon found out, no one in their right mind walks around with over $1,000 cash in their pocket. We had to change our strategy.

In a frenzy, we started buying up other people's more affordable tickets and selling those. Instead of making one big profit, we made a series of smaller ones. Eventually, we recouped our $800 investment, used our glass tickets for ourselves, and enjoyed playoff hockey for free.

This experience would prove useful to me over and over again in life. As Mike Tyson famously said, "Everyone has a plan until they get punched in the mouth." As an entrepreneur, you have to be flexible and think on your feet. Make Plan A, but be prepared to execute Plan B.

9. Embracing My Inner Coach

I REVERED COACHES as a kid, but something stopped me from becoming one myself as I got older. *Coaching is mentorship, and I'm too young to mentor anyone*, my voice of doubt would tell me. *I'm no John Swanson.*

Luckily, a different voice started chiming in. *Why not jump in right now? Coaches have helped you so much; it's time to give back and get involved.*

In college, I started coaching a youth basketball team. We only played once a week, so it was a great way to get my feet wet. My junior year, someone from my Minneapolis traveling basketball team called me about taking over as head coach of the Mankato East eighth-grade traveling basketball team. I said yes almost before the question had been asked, and my first call was to Coach Swanson.

77

"Hey, John, I'm coaching a traveling basketball team. What system should I run?"

"Flex," he answered without skipping a beat.

Flex consisted of an endless pattern of passing and picking, similar to the triangle offense in the NBA. I had run it as a point guard on Swanson's teams, so I knew how to employ it as a coach. I also tapped other Swanson strategies, like making my team play at a fast pace, pressing the entire game and taking every fast-break opportunity. I loved it. My team never let up, and we won most of our games. I did my share of yelling and screaming on the sidelines, but I learned that my authentic coaching style wasn't quite as crazy as my mentor's. :)

In hindsight, coaching youth basketball while also attending college full time and operating a travel business was a bit nuts. My team practiced Tuesday and Thursday nights and played three or four games nearly every weekend — sometimes hours away. I would coach from October to March, then head to Mazatlán as soon as the season ended. I'm not sure how I found the time to juggle all these activities, but I loved every minute of it.

My senior year, I took a different coaching position. By sheer luck, I was assigned to serve as a student teacher for two local coaching legends. One had been a starting quarterback for the University of Minnesota in the 1960s. The other was his son, who had been a backup quarterback for Lou Holtz's Minnesota Golden Gophers football squads.

The father/son duo coached football at a nearby high school, and when they invited me to be an assistant coach for the junior varsity football team, I jumped at the chance. I felt like I was at the top of my game, and I looked the part when I showed up to practices driving a red Jaguar convertible. (I was actually borrowing the car from the owner of the spring break travel business, but that didn't stop the coaches from constantly busting my chops.)

I could fill a separate book with the insights I gained from them and the other coaches in my life, but here are some of the top lessons that have always stayed with me.

My sixth-grade traveling basketball team coach taught me the importance of generosity and being mission based. Behind the scenes, he raised money to fund a summer basketball operation that changed my life and the lives of so many other young boys. Knowing that my mom couldn't afford my travel, he also subsidized my participation. He was an excellent salesman who made things happen, lowered barriers and got people involved.

The two young men who coached my eighth-grade basketball team were right out of college and struck me as just two cool guys hanging out, partying and coaching. I'm not a partier (I don't even drink coffee), but I appreciated that even though they set expectations low and had us play in B-level tournaments, they also taught me that coaching should be fun. I might not have coached youth basketball in college if they hadn't made it seem like a normal thing to do at that age.

John Swanson coached my ninth-grade basketball and eighth-grade football teams, and he stands apart as the primary influence in my life. From him, I learned to raise the bar. Swanson was always on fire. He swore and ripped into his teams. He wasn't afraid to call you "soft." He immediately had us play in high-level tournaments, and he led us to a conference championship.

Swanson was about intensity, high expectations and giving back. He was an attorney by trade. He didn't have to coach, but he did, and he never phoned it in. Some volunteers have a good heart and the right motivations, but they lack passion for the job. Swanson was cut from a different cloth. He pushed me and others to excellence, and he gave us the drive to work harder than we knew we could.

Swanson also taught me the importance of seeing and encouraging your players. When he told me that I'd be a great football player even when I was getting run over by boys twice my size, I trusted him. He also used to tell me that I was smart, and I felt like he was the first person in my life who recognized how my mind worked. I was the kind of player who would enter the huddle and say, "Look, this is what their defense is doing. If we make this adjustment, we'll score." Swanson saw that and encouraged it.

In many ways, my high school football coach was Swanson's opposite: 100% unconditional love. Coach A was relaxed and positive by nature. He showed me how to keep life in perspective and not take the game too seriously — an invaluable lesson when you're a maniac on the field like I was. I needed coaches who cared about me as a person but also pushed me as hard as possible. Looking back, I was lucky to experience both high-energy and laid-back personalities.

Today, I respect coaches and other leaders who create positive cultures. The best locker rooms — not the best individual athletes — win championships. I also respect the "just do your job" philosophies of famous coaches like Bill Belichick and Nick Saban. Their teams won because every player adopted a team mindset. In sports, as in life, you can't win with a "me" attitude. You hear a lot of athletes say things like "Why didn't I start?" "Why'd they take me out of the game?" "Why did *he* get to take the last shot instead of me?" I got caught up in that attitude before I quit my basketball team, and I learned that it's a dead end.

I've done tons of business coaching and look forward to doing a lot more. But aside from some of my daughter's soccer teams, I haven't coached sports since my college days. I'll get back into it when the right opportunity comes around. For now, I'm focused on being at Victoria's current games and cheering her on. I hope my experience as a player and coach shows her and others — especially kids — how team sports can help you develop as a person.

So many successful leaders played team sports in their youth, and most of them credit their success to coaches who supported, challenged and pushed them. We need more of that.

Core Value: Generosity, Owning It

Coaching is a form of generosity by definition, but my coaches went above and beyond. When you're young and struggling in other areas of your life, nothing is more powerful than an adult seeing your potential, giving you a positive outlet, and teaching you the values of teamwork and accountability. Paying that back by doing my own coaching has been even more rewarding.

Did you have a coach who inspired you and gave you confidence as a kid?

Any kind of mentorship has a huge impact. In what ways can you coach someone personally or professionally to pay it forward?

ARMS
OUT

10. Learning from False Starts: Life After College

EARNING MY COLLEGE degree didn't come easily, partly because I had chosen to create so much extra work for myself. But it still felt like a major accomplishment. The only other college graduate in my family was Grandma Phyllis, the same woman who started the neighborhood coupon business. As students and entrepreneurs, we were a team of two.

I had spent my college years in a state of chronic overextension. Few people thought I would cross the finish line, and I understood why. I'd helped run a business. I'd coached multiple youth sports teams. And I had two huge academic barriers: physiology and calculus.

I had no problem with most of my academic subjects, but

physiology killed me, and I had to pass it to graduate. The first two times I took it, the same pattern played out: I would flunk a few tests leading up to the deadline when you could drop a class without affecting your GPA, then I'd drop it. With my advisor's approval, I finally found a summer class at a community college where the credits would transfer back. I studied until my brain nearly exploded, and I passed with a C-minus.

Calculus was the second thorn. Math came easily to me, but I missed the more complex areas because I changed schools so often. I wasn't yet ready for a college-level calculus course, so I followed the same "flunk and drop" pattern I did with physiology. Eventually, I put my head down, focused and earned an A in a summer class.

Not feeling like I needed the public recognition (that might come as a shock to some), I chose not to walk at my college graduation. That decision made my family and friends even *more* skeptical that I'd actually earned my degree, and Grandma Phyllis even jokingly demanded to see my diploma. To this day, I still have nightmares that I never graduated from college. I'll wake up with my heart beating out of my chest, thinking *I still have to pass physiology and calculus!*

On the positive side, one class stayed with me because the professor showed me what it looks like to truly love what you do. "Pop Music, U.S.A." was taught by Professor Aloisio. It covered the entire history of popular music, from the early 1800s to the present, and what I remember is how Professor Aloisio taught it with such infectious passion, sometimes singing and dancing while he taught. The first question he put on every test was: "Music is _____." The answer was "a stimulus," and I've never forgotten that. "Music is a stimulus."

That simple sentence also gave me an invaluable insight into my father. In addition to playing guitar, he wrote music. Knowing this deep connection to his "stimulus" makes his alcoholism and early death even more tragic, but I take comfort in knowing that something made him happy.

My own happiness now rested on figuring out what I was going to do with my life. I loved education, but I didn't want to be a teacher in the traditional K–12 system. I loved teaching, but not the administrative and other aspects of the job. I could have taken a corporate position like many of my friends, but that didn't appeal to me, either. I had to find something else.

My first idea was to stay in the travel industry. I started my own LLC. John Swanson did the paperwork (he was a lawyer, after all). And I partnered with one of the people who had worked for me in the spring break business. I wanted to keep the momentum going from my previous success, but the timing was bad. Websites like Priceline and Travelocity popped up, and many of the discount airlines we had used went out of business. The Kenny Rogers Rule reared its head: Time to fold 'em.

My next LLC was a livestream business called BarTube. *Want to see if you like a band before heading out to see them? Check out BarTube!* I was convinced that consumers would appreciate being able to check out a bar scene before committing to it — especially at a music bar. Musician friends taught me how to tie a Logitech camera into a soundboard, and I used huge computer towers to stream from a handful of bars in the days of low internet bandwidth.

BarTube was ahead of its time as a concept, but too many issues held it back as a viable business. What if someone thinks the bar is dead because the band isn't playing at the exact time they log on? Should I loop footage to give them a better sense of the energy and performance, and can I still call it a "live feed" if I do that? What if a viewer sees one of their colleagues and thinks, "Why aren't they at work?" Interestingly, I recently came across an article about a new app that's causing controversy because it lets users watch people at bars and nightclubs in San Francisco to see if they want to go there. The people in those bars aren't happy about being recorded without their permission.

Ideas don't pay the rent, so I eventually took a full-time job at a large company in the water systems industry. Not surprisingly, I was put in sales — not on the consumer side of the business, but on the commercial side, which meant selling to builders.

The company owner and I liked each other instantly, and I couldn't have been more excited to start that job. But it was a suicide mission. In addition to being the only commercial rep at the company, I was replacing an experienced woman who had taken her builder relationships with her to a competitor. I had no existing customer base and virtually no prospects.

Still, I did everything I could. I'd pack my car with cases of branded water and drive out to model homes. The actual builder was rarely there, so I'd find their real estate agent or builder rep, and our exchanges would go something like this:

"Hey, is the builder around? I just want to drop off some free water."

"Just leave it there," they'd say without looking at me. And I'd never hear from them again.

Unlike my previous sales experiences, this one presented a climb so steep that it was vertical. With no established relationships, I was trying to sell a $15K–$20K product for custom homes under construction. This is one of the first expenses builders cut. Most install cheaper systems to save construction costs, then let the homeowners foot the bill for a better one after they discover how hard their water is.

I lasted a year and a half at the company, and I'm not exaggerating when I say that I didn't sell a single system to a builder. Kenny Rogers started singing in my head again, and it was time to fold 'em. On the upside, I gained invaluable knowledge about luxury customer service and saw what big-time success looks like.

The company had given me tickets in the Minnesota Wild Club section at a time when the Wild were a new hockey franchise and the hottest ticket in town. If there was a builder-related event in the arena, I'd go there between periods.

For a city kid who grew up in government housing, watching local builders and their vendors mix and mingle in a VIP club was like taking a starving man to an all-you-can-eat buffet. *Ten years ago, I was chopping down trees for money and heat. Now I'm standing in a room packed wall-to-wall with high-profile businesspeople!* Those experiences opened the doors to a new world. As a result, new doors began opening in my mind.

Want to live a more Arms Out life? You're not alone! Use the QR code below to register for our FREE newsletter. It's a great way to take your inspiration to the next level.

Core Value: Learning, Staying Positive

My first real sales job could have been a disaster. But instead of beating myself up about not making any sales, I stuck with it, stayed positive and learned what I could.

Have you ever been in what felt like a dead-end career and wanted to quit? Conversely, have you ever stuck with a career and had it turn into a valuable experience?

What's the best example you can think of where you "turned lemons into lemonade"?

Always Learning (Books)

As the saying goes: "Leaders read." Experience is the greatest teacher, but you need more than that. You need to challenge your assumptions and learn something new every day. Great podcasts pop up all the time, but I'm still a book guy. In addition to the works of Zig Ziglar and Jim Rohn, here are the top books that have educated and inspired me along my journey:

- *Extreme Ownership: How U.S. Navy SEALs Lead and Win* (Jocko Willink and Leif Babin). The book that saved me from ever falling into a victim mentality, and one of the reasons why "Owning It" is one of my Core Values.

- *Think and Grow Rich* (Napoleon Hill). A great book on the power of positivity coupled with action. You need both.

- *The Shadow Effect: Illuminating the Hidden Power of Your True Self Through Comprehensive and Practical Shadow Work* (Deepak Chopra, Debbie Ford and Marianne Williamson). The pages written by Debbie Ford are some of the most unbelievable words you'll ever read about embracing every part of you to become a complete human being.

- *The 5 Levels of Leadership and the 21 Irrefutable Laws of Leadership* (John C. Maxwell). The blueprints for leading a team — any team — when you're ready to take the plunge. Anything by John Maxwell is worth reading.

- *The Five Dysfunctions of a Team* (Patrick Lencioni). The next critical book to read on your leadership journey.

- *Atomic Habits: An Easy & Proven Way to Build Good Habits & Break Bad Ones* (James Clear). A great reminder that being an effective leader isn't magic. It's hard work that requires you to get a little better every day.

- *Good to Great: Why Some Companies Make the Leap … and Others Don't* (Jim Collins). Collins' description of a Level 5 Leader as someone who displays a mixture of strong will, humility and a bigger purpose has always stayed with me.

- *The 7 Habits of Highly Effective People* (Stephen R. Covey). It was first published over 35 years ago, but it's still in the Mount Rushmore of business books for me.

- *How to Win Friends and Influence People* (Dale Carnegie). The winner and still champion. Every motivational book written since is just riffing on it.

11. Real Estate Offers a Home

I DIDN'T KNOW many people in the real estate industry, and I had never thought about becoming an agent. I did, however, empathize with people who struggled to find housing. Moving so often as a kid had ingrained the importance of "home" in my bones. For some, a house is an important investment. For others, it's a matter of life and death.

So many of my childhood challenges revolved around shelter: having to move out after my parents' separation, struggling to survive in Brian's primitive Pequot Lakes cabin, being teased for living in an apartment. In hindsight, I'm grateful that my mother made sure we always had a place to live. Back then, I often wondered why our family couldn't live in a nice single-family home and just be "normal."

After I left the water company, I entered a deeply unstable job market. This was 2008–09. The country was experiencing the worst recession in a generation, and an imploding housing market was dragging the entire economy down with it. Property values were in free fall.

One day, an attorney friend told me about an interesting trend with foreclosures in suburban/exurban developments. Builders were developing and selling half their properties, then using the money to build even more. They were essentially living on credit, which works when home values go up, but not when prices plunge. Builders were now stuck with thousands of half-finished homes, and the finance companies who had lent the money between banks and builders were left holding the bag.

"The finance companies are hiring me to clean up their mess," my friend told me. "If you get your real estate license, you can help me sell all these homes." *This guy's going to hand me a book of business!* I thought. After my water company experience, that sounded like a dream scenario, so I jumped into real estate with my usual over-the-top enthusiasm.

The state required 90 hours of classes to earn your license — a number I now find ridiculously low — and the entire process usually took six to eight weeks. I did it in half the time. In just a few weeks, I was a licensed real estate agent. I immediately called my attorney friend.

"Let's go!" I said, eager to get my hands on all that business he had promised me. Silence. He gave me a long story about why things weren't quite ready on his end and told me to be patient. When this pattern repeated itself over the next few weeks and months, I realized that our business partnership was never going to happen.

This experience was another disappointment, but I had a new asset: my real estate license. I wanted to continue in the business, but I was in no hurry. When you're in your early 20s, done with school and free of debt (thanks to my college business ventures), life is all about you. I was also dating a young woman named Rachel at the time, so I thought I could relax and take some time to figure out my next move.

I was wrong.

———————————

Core Values: Learning, Staying Positive

Earning my real estate license was a learning process I fully embraced. I quickly realized that it was a good industry for me, and I wanted to keep learning more. After the disappointment of not getting the job I expected, I stayed positive and planned on further exploring the business.

Did you ever take a class in school that you took a surprising interest in? Did you pursue that passion or let it go?

Why do you work in your current industry? Is it purely practical, something you're good at, a true passion, or all three?

12. A Phone Call Changes Everything

MY PHONE RANG while I was looking at new clubs in the middle of a golf store.

"Hello?"

"Hey, where are you? Can you come home?" said Rachel.

"I'm buying a club and then golfing with some buddies," I said, somewhat annoyed that she would interrupt this sacred guy activity. "What's up?"

"Um, we're having a baby?"

My stomach dropped. I probably also dropped the putter I was holding. My mind went blank as I struggled to take in the words I had just heard.

"I'll come home right away!"

"No, keep your plans," Rachel said. "We can talk later. I just needed to tell you as soon as I found out."

I kept the golf date, but I was a mess. I couldn't tell my buddies the news because it was too fresh. But eight holes in, I was so out of it that they kept asking me if I was okay. I assured them I was, but I made up an excuse to leave.

On the drive home, I realized how quickly I needed to grow up. I thought about how my siblings and I were raised: The money struggles. The constant moves. The new schools and friends. The verbal and physical violence. Some people repeat their parents' mistakes, as if the only way to make others feel their pain is to inflict it on them. Others overcorrect, and their kids never learn how to become adults. What kind of father was I going to be? All I could think was: *You have to do better than your dad. For starters, put that real estate license to work and get a job.*

I found a brokerage and went to work.

Looking back, I owe a huge debt of gratitude to Rachel's father, Brad, who was a real estate entrepreneur. Day one as an agent can be disorienting. Up to that point, you're only focused on getting through classes and passing tests. Then you hit the real world and think, *I'm in an office, I'm on my own, and there's no one to help me.* As a top-producing agent at multiple brokerages, Brad knew real estate inside and out, and no one did more in my early days to help me learn.

Some people repeat their parents' mistakes, as if the only way to make others feel their pain is to inflict it on them. Others overcorrect, and their kids never learn how to become adults. What kind of father was I going to be? All I could think was: You have to do better than your dad.

In the traditional, big-brokerage real estate model, you have to blaze your own path because other agents see you as a competitor. This didn't strike me as the best approach, but I knew how to do things on my own. Brad didn't hand me a book of business, because he knew it wouldn't help me in the long run. But he told me that I was a quick study and told others that I was smart, both of which boosted my confidence. He also encouraged me to create the business *I* wanted, focusing on marketing, convenience and scaling up.

As for getting customers, I had to start at the bottom like everyone else, with "floor duty." In 2009, floor duty consisted of signing up for certain times where you'd be in your brokerage's office, usually for an entire month. If a random person stopped by the office or called in and said they were looking to sell or buy a house, you'd get the opportunity. It felt like fishing without bait, and I sat on floor duty for 25 days with no action.

Then I got a bite. A commercial construction guy walked in, pointed to a listing and said, "Take me to see this residential lot." He was all business. I was all enthusiasm.

"Let's go!" I said. I grabbed the plat map of the area — a diagram showing how the lot was divided into different properties. I had never shown a piece of land to anyone, and no one had trained me on how to read a plat map. Like people just starting out in any business, I assumed I would just "figure it out."

The client followed me up to the development, and as we walked down a cul-de-sac toward the area in question, he started asking me detailed questions I didn't have a clue about.

"What can you tell me about the well and septic setbacks?"

"Um … " I squinted as I held the plat map upside down.

"Hey, Kris, the lot's over here."

"Oh, yeah." I subtly turned the map over. My client had been in construction for decades and had the vocabulary I lacked. I had no idea what I was doing, and I wasn't hiding it very well. In moments like these, it's important not to panic. Just try to be helpful in any way you can. That's what I did, and the client appreciated it — either that or he was just a nice guy who felt sorry for me. Either way, he eventually walked to his truck, came back holding a piece of paper and said the three magic words every real estate agent loves to hear:

"I'll take it."

Before I knew it, I was staring at a check for $49,000. It was the most money I had ever seen.

"Awesome. Thanks!" I said. I didn't know what to do with

the check. I didn't know how to draft a land contract. And I didn't have any paperwork with me. I told the guy I'd get everything taken care of, and I called my manager the second I returned to the office.

"This guy wants to buy a lot, and he gave me a check for the full amount!" I said, a bit excited. "I need contracts or purchase agreements, right?" My manager laughed because a land deal is more complicated than a regular home sale. It's not the ideal first transaction for an agent, but it was my first closing, and I swelled with pride.

My second sale was more traditional, and it exposed even more of my knowledge gaps. As I showed a suburban split-level, my engineer client peppered me with questions inside the mechanical room. Unless you have a construction background, this is the last room you want to enter as an agent. Based on my water company experience, I could talk about water softeners. But that was it. *How do I get out of here as fast as possible?* I thought, along with: *You really need to educate yourself on mechanical rooms.*

Luckily, I still made the sale.

Most memories of my early agent days involve getting lost. Garmin GPS devices existed, as did a less sophisticated version of Google Maps, but neither could recognize new developments or construction sites. After typing in a property's address, I'd sometimes end up three or four towns away. I whipped a lot of U-turns in those days, and I would drive with a pit in my stomach as a customer followed me to a site when I had no clue where I was going.

Confusion and uncertainty can lead some people to quit,

but no matter what industry you're in, situations like these are usually far worse in your head than they are in reality. I quickly learned that people can be forgiving if they sense that you truly care about them. I also learned that if you're trying to help people, you need to lead, not follow — especially when it comes to working with couples in real estate. Ask the right questions up front and avoid the "he said/she said" cycle where you're playing middleman between couples who haven't hashed out their own differences. (More on that later.)

My childhood had demanded resilience, and I refused to let intimidation or embarrassment limit me. Keeping with the pattern I started when I tried out for that fourth-grade wrestling team, I figured things out on the fly and focused on being helpful, not perfect. I was especially sensitive not to waste people's time. I remember thinking: *This industry could serve customers a lot better, and don't people deserve a better experience for the commissions they're paying? How can you change an industry so set in its ways to be more convenient and customer-centric?*

I was new to this world, but my brain bubbled with ideas on how to make it better. Problem was, I couldn't act on any of these visions until I had listings. Oh, and I also had a baby on the way. No pressure …

Core Values: Learning, Staying Positive

Discovering that I was about to be a father brought my life into sharp focus. I had to hit the ground running as a real estate agent and learn as I went. The key to surviving this period of my life was staying positive. All I could do was try to help people, even when my knowledge and experience fell short. By doing that, I learned that people will give you the benefit of the doubt if they sense that you care and are doing your best to help them.

When have you been thrown into a situation where you felt completely over your head? Did you keep at it, or did you get frustrated and quit?

Do you find that you give people more rope when you sense that they truly care about helping you, even if they're not perfect?

The house I briefly lived in as a child before my parents separated and could no longer afford it.

The activity that has been with me throughout my life,
from leaky johnboats to outings with Tony Capra.

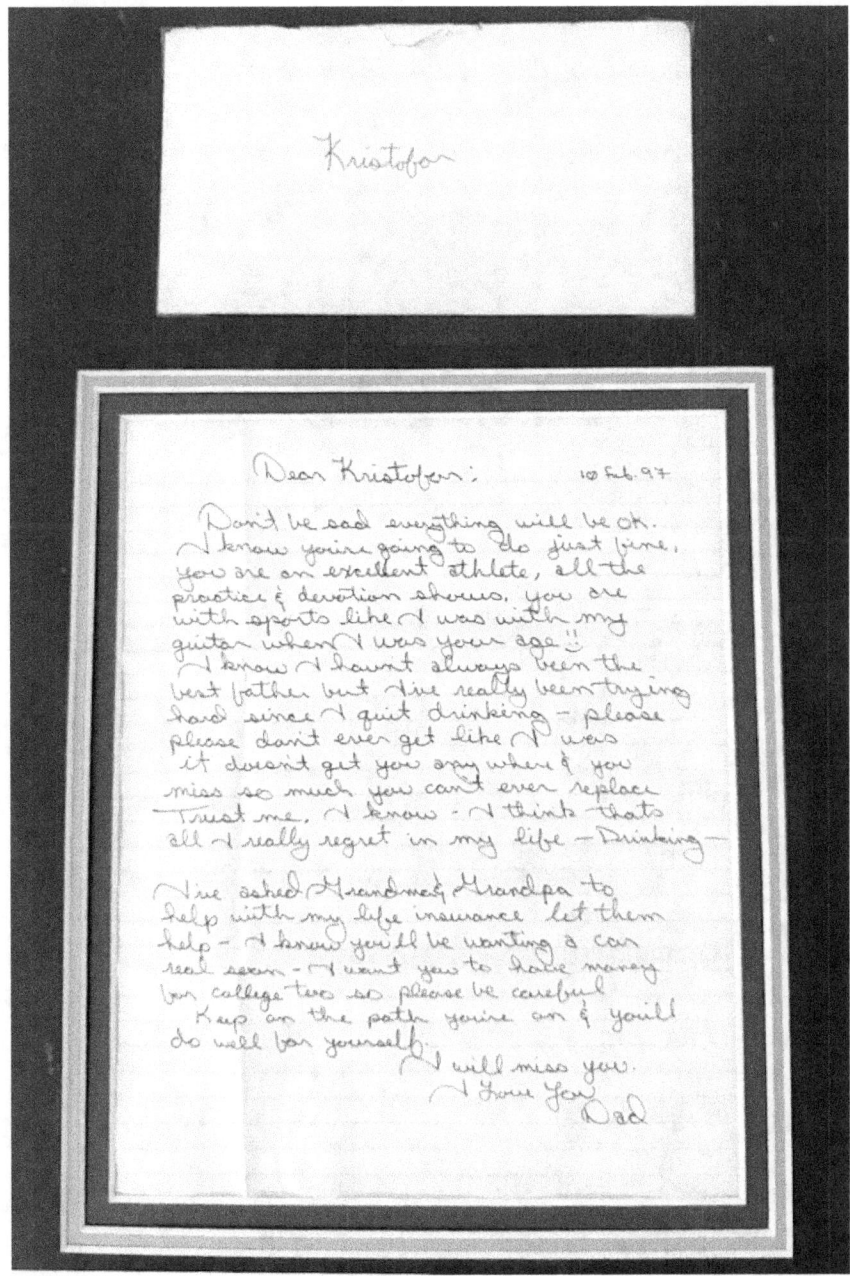

My dad's letter to me when he was in a moment of sobriety and reflection. He wrote similar letters to my siblings.

The social media challenge that quickly got out of hand, but also taught me a valuable lesson in using your platform for good.

NEXT PAGE: *My dad's memorial flyer.*

John

John's death certificate reads "killed in a non-accidental manner from blunt force injuries," due to alcohol and rage.

When his body was dislodged from the undercarriage of the impact vehicle he was left with a crushed thorax and many other mutilating injuries. He lived on for 7 hours while surgeons tried to clean him internally and rebuild his shattered body. Although they tried desperately to bring him back too much damage had been done and he died.

John's children were the love of his life and now they are fatherless. They have missed his being part of their school activities, proms and graduations that were so special and important to him.

His daughter tells how she misses her dad composing special songs on his guitar just for her, his special "Baby Doll." His son's miss fishing trips, sporting events and just being together.

John had a life so full of potential in music, electronics, making the rank of Captain in the military and all the future wonders life holds. Because his body was mutilated today he is ashes. John's death was totally preventable.

An image from my dad's deployment to Norway. He thought he was going to Iraq and might never come back.

Hanging out with great friends and colleagues. Above from left: Darin Dawson, Gary Ashton and Justin Havre. Below from left: Justin, Gary and Jon Cheplak.

The photo that launched a brand and a movement.

The billboard that Rachel and Victoria surprised me with in 2018.

My nephew showing me how it's done.

My family of strong and wonderful women
… and don't forget Ollie!

ARMS OUT

13. Finding Opportunity

WHEN YOU'RE NEW to an industry, you see it with fresh eyes. And when foreclosures exploded during the economic recession of 2008–2009, I took a hard look at Housing and Urban Development (HUD) homes.

HUD is a massive federal government agency, and back then they owned a large share of the houses that were entering foreclosure. These properties were often trashed and would sit vacant for months. After HUD took them back, the agents who got the listings would treat them as exclusive. Then they'd resell the homes without doing much to improve them or clean them up.

After researching the relationship between HUD and these agents, I learned something surprising: Their agreements back then weren't exclusive at all; they were open-listing contracts. In other words, certain real estate agents thought they had the exclusive right to sell HUD properties, but they didn't. Other agents like me were 100% free to advertise them as well. With no inventory of my own, I decided to break what I saw as an artificial stranglehold on HUD listings. I didn't just dip my toe in the water. I cannonballed into the pool.

Craigslist was relatively new back then, and it was one of the best technology tools around. Seeing a huge opportunity, I developed a marketing system that worked as follows:

- Grab some photos of the HUD listing.

- Enter the number of bedrooms and bathrooms, etc.

- Go to a free website at the time where landlords, property managers, real estate agents and homeowners could advertise properties for sale.

- Paste HTML code directly into the body of a Craigslist post (which was *the* place to be before the big real estate portals came along).

- Wait for the inquiries to come in.

I was basically inundating Craigslist with digital flyers for HUD properties with *my* name attached, and it worked better than I could have imagined. My phone buzzed all day long with buyers saying, "Hey, I'm looking at 123 Main Street on Craigslist. What can you tell me about it?"

As you can imagine, the established HUD agents were less

than thrilled with me. Just as I had irritated the Goliath spring break company in college, I had invaded what they saw as their terrain, even though it wasn't. My phone also buzzed with calls from *them*, and the conversations went something like this:

"Hey, lay off my listings!"

"They're not your listings. They're open listings."

"No, they're not. They've always been mine!"

"If you have a different contract with HUD than what I'm seeing, then I'd be happy to call them and ask about it."

The calls usually ended there. The agents knew that the facts were on my side. I forced them to acknowledge an unfair advantage that was hurting consumers by limiting competition.

On the downside, Craigslist eventually started tracking IP addresses to prevent people from being as aggressive as I was. If I posted there more than 10 times in a day, they'd make me wait another 24 hours before posting again. I didn't stop there, of course. Consumers loved my system, so I created computer towers for about $300 each and set them up in friends' and family members' homes. I shut off "standby" and "sleep" on the towers to keep them running 24/7. I bought software to give each one its own IP address. And I installed remote-access software so an admin from anywhere in the world could log in and post to Craigslist from that IP address.

At one point, I had nine of these towers sending my listings to Craigslist from nine different IP addresses. I ran this system for a couple of years, even taking the time to personally restart each tower every month or two after it ran out of memory. The effort was worth it: My business grew so fast that I built up enough money to hire an overseas team to scale my system even bigger.

When the big real estate technology companies entered the market (the ones that still dominate as I write this), they started syndicating listings data, giving my system the equivalent of compound interest. My distribution tripled, and my phone nearly exploded.

Next, I created my own system for measuring and optimizing results. I tracked the correlation between having a listing at the top of Craigslist and receiving a call for that property. The big insight: The second a listing fell down the page, the call volume dropped. In the internet age, the key to victory would be getting to the top of every list.

Looking back, I realize that I was living in a Wild West period. New frontiers opened up in real estate technology and aggregator services nearly every day, and I thrived in that wide-open environment. Consumers were sending a clear message that they preferred these systems. They loved the convenience. They loved the speed. And they appreciated anyone who understood their behavior and responded to their needs.

If you find yourself seeing a new world that others in your industry don't, it's your gain and their loss. In my case, I would let other agents keep handing out calendars and refrigerator magnets. I was going to take full advantage of every new technology in my industry.

> *"If you find yourself seeing a new world that others in your industry don't, it's your gain and their loss."*

I quickly built enough inventory to attract buyers. Now I needed to take the next big step, and that came when I attended a seminar on short sales. I knew these kinds of events well: A speaker would make a process sound so complex that you felt like you had no choice but to hire them to handle it for you. I don't remember the exact title of the seminar, but it should have been called "Just Give Me All Your Short-Sale Listings."

Millions of Americans were underwater in their mortgages back then. To make properties easier to sell, banks and other lenders were sometimes willing to take lower mortgage payoffs than the consumer owed. That's what a short sale involves, and the seminar speaker wanted to make it sound as complicated as possible.

It seemed straightforward to me, so my first thought was *I can do short sales better than this guy.* I saw it from an emotional perspective. Homeowners in short-sale situations feel vulnerable and need help. They want someone to simplify the process for them and make it work as smoothly as possible. Ultimately, getting that sale comes down to driving traffic to a website.

I decided to dominate the short-sale market in my area. Winning people over in any industry starts with serving as a resource rather than a salesperson. Give people something of value, and they'll more than likely give you something back. It's fundamental human behavior.

Consumers didn't have a guide for short-sale situations, so one of my first moves was to write "A Homeowner's Guide to Short Sales" and mail it to a list of homeowners who would likely appreciate the help. Unlike the seminar speaker I had seen, I was there to make the process feel easier, not harder. My message to each book recipient was simple and non-aggressive: "Here's a resource for when the time is right." And it worked.

Today, aspects of what I did with this campaign would be called "content marketing," "educating the consumer," "soft-selling," "thought leadership" and "lead-magnet generation." I didn't know any of those terms. I just knew that thousands of people in my market were upside down on their mortgages. Short-selling was their best option. And educating them was the right thing to do.

Knowing the importance of being first on Google and other websites, I also dove headfirst into search engine optimization. Like so many other aspects of technology, SEO existed in a primitive form back then. I was so focused on driving traffic that I went online and hired so-called outside "SEO experts" to help. I trusted them with a niche short-sale website, and I initially had success with their strategies. Soon, though, I learned that their tactics were geared for short-term, not long-term, success. Lesson learned, I brought SEO in-house and put significant work into KrisLindahl.com, which now is one of the country's top branded real estate websites.

My main takeaway from this experience, which applies to any industry, was the 80/20 rule. The vast majority of people responded well to my outreach and educational efforts. A small minority didn't, and I didn't let them stop me. I went with the majority and kept offering value when they needed it. As a result, appointments flew in because I was the guy who wrote the book on short sales and understood what they were going through. I was sometimes signing eight listing packages in a single day.

Within a year of attending that short-sale seminar, I was my state's top short-sale agent. After noticing that so many buyers of my bank-mediated listings were investors, I also learned the value of investing in real estate to build wealth — something that would soon become core to my business and life, and still is.

I was proud of my grit and success in these early days, but I wasn't happy with something else. Many of you reading this book will identify with it no matter what profession you're in: My work environment didn't feel right. Should I leave it or try to change it?

Core Values: Learning, Tenacity

When my back was against the wall, I looked for opportunities to succeed and went after them hard. From breaking a false monopoly to using the latest technologies, I was (and continue to be) tenacious about using any tool that shows consumers you understand their needs and are willing to help them through difficult situations.

I also learned from the real estate investors who bought my short-sale listings. I was helping these people build wealth. Why wouldn't I do that for myself as well?

Are you someone who likes to break the mold and ask forgiveness instead of permission, or are you risk-averse?

In your professional life, are you more focused on pleasing people internally or meeting the customer's needs?

Every Detail Counts

When our agents asked homeowners to remember the company and agent on the last 10 yard signs they'd seen, almost no one could do it. When asked "would you rather have a sign that stands out or looks like everyone else's?" they voted for one that stands out.

The message was clear: Consumer behaviors and expectations have changed, yet the yard sign sits frozen in time: 20 x 30 or 18 x 24 inches, brokerage logo, URL, phone number. Boring.

I decided to reinvent the yard sign, but I had no idea how hard it would be.

The vision seemed simple enough: Use a die-cut version of the Arms Out image within a dual-post system with a crossbar (instead of one beam), add a brochure holder, use QR codes, and include the message "Open House: All Day, Every Day" to show that we thought traditional open houses were outdated.

Problem was, the world was in the thick of a pandemic, and vinyl — not to mention grommets and hooks — was harder to find than toilet paper. The vinyl wholesalers we

125

talked to told us we'd have to wait 12–18 months and pay up to 10 times the normal cost.

In the end, we had to start our own sign manufacturing division. We locked up the vinyl inventories at every home improvement store in town (paying retail, which was actually cheaper than wholesale). Then we handled every detail, from sending trucks to pick up the supplies, to manufacturing the signs, marking the utility lines in the yard, installing during all seasons, you name it.

The ultimate detail: We knew that most cities require yard signs to be no more than 6 square feet in size. This was based on the fact that most are 20 inches x 30 inches. Our design was radically different from the typical rectangle, but to avoid problems with municipalities, we made sure that our signs were engineered on CAD to be 5.99 square feet in size.

Lesson learned: Vision is important, but it means nothing if you can't execute down to the tiniest detail.

14. An Entrepreneur Stuck in a Corporate Environment

I JOINED A large brokerage to learn the complexities of real estate within an established institution, but I quickly discovered my personality wasn't right for a corporate environment. The energy felt low. Agents didn't trust each other. No one seemed as curious or obsessive as I was about the people who mattered most: customers.

I learned that large corporate brokerages use their agents largely as marketing tools — to put up yard signs that grow their brand. Yet these brokerages have almost no control over the actual consumer experience, because that's determined by each individual agent, one relationship at a time.

I also learned that, while real estate agents generally

receive too much credit in a hot market and too much blame in a cold one, complacency and entitlement ruled when I started. Before the economic meltdown, most agents had been living the high life. "Sold in Two Minutes!" their ads would shout, as if they were solely responsible for the speed of every home sale. Now that the market had ground to a halt, were agents holding themselves accountable for *that*? No.

Once I got my bearings, I felt like a restless entrepreneur trapped in a corporate setting. I questioned everything. I stirred the pot. I felt like things should be different. I didn't want to blindly follow the rules; I wanted to challenge the ones that didn't make sense.

I fixated on customer service, because that's the Achilles' heel in so many industries. While companies like Amazon, Google and Apple scored victory after victory by being more customer-centric than their competitors, real estate agents kept playing from the same old playbook while making relatively high commissions.

In my day-to-day life, I focused on people and relationships. For example, one day I drove to a suburban house to explore a potential short sale and stepped into total chaos — stuff everywhere, kids crawling up the walls. Something was clearly off. The husband didn't want to talk to me, and his wife kept telling him to "sit down so we can get this over with." I could tell that they were in financial trouble. The wife knew it, but her husband was in denial. They were so hostile to each other that when a delivery person showed up with half a dozen pizzas, the wife grabbed the top box and threw it at her husband. Literally *threw* it at him!

"You know what?" I said, standing up from the kitchen

table. "I don't think we're ready to have this conversation yet. I'll come back when you're on the same page."

"I fixated on customer service because that's the Achilles' heel in so many industries. While companies like Amazon, Google and Apple scored victory after victory by being more customer-centric than their competitors, real estate agents kept playing from the same old playbook while making relatively high commissions."

Some agents ignore people's real problems. When I walk into a toxic scene like this, I'm not afraid to bring up bigger issues. "I don't think this is about selling your house," I might say. "Tell me why I'm *really* here today." I also wasn't afraid to tell people who overvalued their properties that while I could create the best marketing and use the best technology in the world, I couldn't wave a magic wand and make someone buy their house. It's like dealing with an addict: You can send them to rehab a million times, but it won't work until *they* want it to.

I didn't know how to do any of this on day one, because no one teaches these skills. Most sales training fixates on "closing the deal," and that's where I started too. My early mindset was about fast success. But I quickly learned that if I left an appointment knowing only that someone wanted to sell their house, I wouldn't earn their business. The more I tapped into the deeper emotions around a home sale, the better I did. My mindset shifted from "how do I sell a house *now*?" to "how do I build a relationship with this person so I can help them out?"

That's not to say I didn't make mistakes along the way, and I still do. When you're a hammer, everything looks like a nail. And when you're a visionary entrepreneur, everything looks like an opportunity.

A perfect example is a business I started as I was building my real estate practice. A college friend (the same one who had owned the Travelmaster RV that we used to sell trips to Mazatlán) had a body shop one state over, and people were always asking him if he had used cars to sell. So we built a

Want to live a more Arms Out life? You're not alone! Use the QR code below to register for our FREE newsletter. It's a great way to take your inspiration to the next level.

website: Tell us the used vehicle you want, we'll find it for you. We built a "What's Your Car Worth?" tool to drive people to it. And we bought 15–20 cars at a big car auction in his state before we had a mechanic to check them out or a plan to get them across the state border.

We immediately got flooded with more leads than we could handle, and the whole project proved to be too much for me. I exited after a year, right around the time a new company turned the automotive world upside down by adopting a similar concept.

> *"When you're a hammer, everything looks like a nail. And when you're a visionary entrepreneur, everything looks like an opportunity."*

I love entrepreneurs, and I love coaching them (to this day, I'll stop at every lemonade stand I see, get to know the kids while I coach them a little, then buy some lemonade and slip them a hundred-dollar bill). But once you start having success as an entrepreneur, you start to believe you can do anything. A recent example: Noticing how many people were interested in how I built my current company's brand, I started a marketing agency to help others build an Inescapable Brand like mine. Soon after I launched it, I realized that I didn't have the time to run both a marketing agency *and* my brokerage, so I shifted to consulting and speaking, which I still do.

In addition to maintaining your focus, a huge key to entrepreneurial success is using your "failures" to get better. I once asked a woman why she and her husband chose a different agent over me, and she said: "My husband had a better connection with the other guy, and we felt like you were talking to me and not him." That was a great lesson. Like most agents, I tended to focus on the alpha — the person who dominates conversation and seems more motivated to move. The quieter member of a couple is often the decision-maker, so I started going back and forth in my conversations with couples. If one person dominated, I would turn to the other, make eye contact and say, "And how do *you* feel?"

Did my upbringing give me an intuitive advantage in

131

building relationships? Probably. As a child, I would absorb the conflict around me and crave answers that were never there. "Why does my dad's behavior get worse the later it gets?" "Why are my parents fighting?" "Why does my grandfather spend so much time with me and not with his own son?" I learned how to read a room. I also learned to be relentless. I loved the pressure of being in close basketball games and wanting to take the last shot, and I still replicate that pressure to bring out my best.

Bottom line: Every industry is emotional. My advantage in business is the fact that I experienced so many big life events at an early age, tapped into my natural intuition and executed at a consistently high level. Seeing a lack of communication in my corporate environment, I also decided early on to become the best communicator possible.

Today, I train my team on the values of communication and relationships. "Get to the confrontation as soon as possible," I tell them. Some people will reveal more to a real estate agent than they will to each other. Even if they hold back, asking good questions helps them reach their next chapter.

When you're talking to a couple, you might hear one person say they absolutely need to sell their house, while the other stays silent. One might insist on having a bigger kitchen, the other on having a bigger garage. One might fixate on the feel of their next home, while the other is pragmatic and insists on exactly three bedrooms and two bathrooms. Get people to talk about the values and emotions behind their needs. Challenge them if you have to.

But I'm getting ahead of myself. In 2011, another powerful

technology was taking off among consumers while being ignored in my industry. I jumped into it headfirst. Big surprise: I had no idea what I was getting myself into.

Core Values: Empathy, Learning, Owning It

I felt restless in a big corporate environment because I was obsessed with figuring out what makes people tick and how to better meet their needs. That attitude — and my upbringing — led me to take an intuitive, empathetic and relentless approach. I also sought feedback and development opportunities so I could keep getting better.

Have you ever felt like a fish out of water in a work environment? What felt wrong to you?

Are you good at receiving and acting on constructive criticism, or do you avoid it?

What efforts do you make to get better at what you do?

ARMS
OUT

15. Cheap Suits & Hostage Videos: Embracing Technology

SMARTPHONES AND SOCIAL media began to take off around the time I started in real estate, and it became clear that the world was about to change forever. Facebook opened to the public in 2006. Apple released its first iPhone in 2007. By 2011, more and more people were glued to their phones, watching videos and posting on social media. Today, we take this behavior for granted. Back then, it was a massive shift.

To anyone paying attention, the potential of video as a marketing tool was obvious. Everyone now had the ability to make and distribute video content for free. Other industries were doing it, but not real estate. Why?

I quickly became a heavy social media user, but I was too

self-conscious to do personal videos. When I finally decided to jump in, I treated video like another sport. *Who cares if I don't know anything about cameras, lighting or how to talk to a lens? I'll blitz the market with dozens of short, customized videos touting myself as the short-sale agent in every major real estate market in the state. Easy, right?*

The execution would prove slightly more complicated.

The first obstacle was money. After investing my limited budget in a tripod and the best DSLR camera I could find, I didn't have much left. I went to Men's Wearhouse to buy a dozen of the cheapest suits I could find. I ordered a set of low-budget lights from eBay that probably violated every fire code ever written. And when I realized that I couldn't afford a green screen or expensive backdrop, I walked onto a bridge in the city, snapped a dozen pictures of the skyline and had the best one printed on a large vinyl sheet.

The second obstacle was fear. Every time I thought I was ready to record, I'd find another thing that wasn't quite right or another item I needed to buy. The vinyl was too creased, so I went to Home Depot to buy clips to stretch it out. The backdrop looked too dark, so I bought another backlight. Eventually, I realized that I was just procrastinating.

The moment of truth arrived when I grabbed a vacant room on the second floor of my brokerage. I set up the camera, flipped on the hot lights and slipped into one of my cheap suits. The HVAC system was so loud that I had to shut it off before recording, which made the lights scorch even more. Not able to afford a teleprompter, I taped a few lines of handwritten copy just below the camera lens. Face dripping with sweat, I finally found the courage to hit Record.

"Hi there. My name is Kris Lindahl. In 2011, I was the #1 short-sale agent within [brokerage]. Are you looking to short-sale your home in [city or town]? If so, I can help. You can visit my short-sale calculator site listed below or call … "

I repeated this routine over and over again, covering hundreds of locations. Between takes, I'd wipe my face, flip the A/C back on, change into a different suit and run into the hallway to make sure no one was listening. I did this for nine hours straight. When I was done, the final files were so huge — and the internet so slow — that uploading them to YouTube (another great new tool) took almost as long as shooting them.

By today's standards, these videos are both terrible and hilarious. I call them my "hostage videos" because you can't help but imagine someone standing off camera and pointing a gun at my head. I knew my delivery was stiff, but I powered through the different locations anyway. I had committed to becoming a great communicator, and this was part of the process. The videos didn't have to be perfect; they just had to exist.

Today, I make videos almost every day. I have a state-of-the-art home video and podcasting studio with multiple cameras, lighting rigs and backdrops. I appear on TV and speak in front of audiences all over the country. When people tell me I'm a "natural," I crack up. Any impression that I'm comfortable speaking on camera or in front of thousands of people is the result of practice. My hostage videos prove how far I've come, and there's still room for improvement.

So what happened when I released my hostage videos into the wild? My phone rang off the hook yet again. What those videos lacked in performance and production values they made up for in authenticity and originality. People appreciated that I was trying something new and reaching them where they were: online. The consumer mindset was: *If this guy is forward-thinking enough to do a video, then he can probably sell my home.* Buyers agreed. They called because I had so many homes to sell.

"Any impression that I'm comfortable speaking on camera or in front of thousands of people is the result of practice. My hostage videos prove how far I've come, and there's still room for improvement."

It helped that I also had a strategy to distribute the videos. I blasted them to every corner of the internet using a third-party service. Because I used key words and phrases (e.g., putting several cities before "short-sale agent"), I once again earned top organic search rankings.

I also opened a digital PR account, which at the time allowed subscribers to buy unlimited digital press release distribution. This was a license to pump out infinite online content, so I hired a writer to churn out releases based on the same topics: short sales in [insert city]. I used the same titles for the releases as I did for the videos, so when people searched online, they'd find consistent video and text-based content followed by a link to my website.

Speaking of my website, I dramatically improved the user experience there by creating a "short-sale calculator." Anyone considering a short sale wanted to know if it made sense financially, so I gave them a convenient tool to find out. Places like the *Harvard Business Review* call techniques like these "gaining a first-mover advantage." At the time, I just thought, *Hey, if I get off to a huge head start with this calculator, other people won't be able to catch up!*

The timing was good because a top real estate tech platform had just released an API code for a popular feature that allowed you to quickly estimate the value of your house. The code was available for real estate agents to use, so I built a consumer calculator/algorithm that cross-referenced different data sets to help people calculate whether or not a short sale might make sense for them. Then I launched ads asking, "Should you short-sale or not?" with links to the calculator.

People ate it up. When they entered their information, our formula compared their mortgage balance against their estimate. If you were considering a short sale, you could find out instantly if you were underwater or not, and by how much. I nearly fainted when I saw how many people used my short-sale calculator in its first 24 hours.

The best part: Our customer outreach didn't stop there. After you got your calculator results, you'd receive an email from me saying something like: "You're –$100,000 on your house, which means a short sale might be the right move for you."

Next, you'd get a call within 60 seconds of the email that was crafted to be helpful and non-aggressive. I made these calls myself initially, then I hired a call center to maintain the quick responsiveness. I made sure to position myself as a resource: "Kris wanted me to give you a call because you just filled out our short-sale calculator. He wanted to make sure you received your report, and he'd love to go over the results with you."

The dots connected overnight, and I could barely keep up with the appointments. I had chosen to educate people because I knew it was the right thing to do. And I offered value because I knew that it would keep them engaged. By the time I showed up at people's homes, I had already earned their trust. They knew that I understood every aspect of short sales and that I was there to help.

Similar calculators started popping up on the internet, and someone eventually created one for agents across the country. I didn't mind. I had already earned the top organic rankings for every city in the state. I was just one agent with an assistant and some outsourced talent, and I was now competing with huge teams at national brokerages with high overhead costs. I'll take that any day.

As I churned out new content, people started using a word to describe me that I heard all the time in my sports days: "Man, that Kris Lindahl guy is relentless!"

This is just the beginning, I thought. Time to scale up.

Core Values: Empathy, Tenacity

Once I started flexing my entrepreneurial muscles, I kept seeing ways to merge empathy with technology. Every new tool inspired me to jump in first and push the boundaries — especially video, which helped me become a better leader, communicator and speaker. But I also never forgot that technology only works when you use it to connect emotionally. People want you to understand their situations, and they want you to educate and help them.

As a consumer, which influencers do you follow on social media?

Have those influencers truly built something and proven their success (vs. simply buying their followers)?

Have you ever bought something from one of them? If so, how did they earn your trust?

Does the influencer content you consume have to be technically perfect, or just original and relevant?

ARMS OUT

16. Bringing the Team Concept to Business

ONE DAY I pulled up to a listing appointment in a Mini Cooper that also served as a mobile billboard for my business. As I got out of the car, the homeowner flashed a big smile and said, "Keep it humble." That was the beginning of a successful transaction and incredible friendship with Mike Paton. Many entrepreneurs know Mike as the former CEO of EOS Worldwide, the company behind the Entrepreneurial Operating System. I was about to know him as one of my most important mentors.

"You have something special," Mike said after I sold his house. "But if you want to scale, you're going to need a solid team around you." Those words changed everything for me. I had spent years watching individual real estate agents scramble to handle everything from staging and photography to advertising and open houses. I had wondered if customers wouldn't be better served by a team of specialists, and Mike validated that idea.

I felt that consumers often received subpar service for the commissions they paid their agents. That was partly due to the fact that these agents were trained by brokerage managers. Most of these managers didn't succeed on the front lines. They gave advice to agents on how to build their business and brand, even though they'd never done it themselves! This is why so many agents continue to want to join our team. They can see the brand we've built.

Despite these shortcomings, consumers didn't demand more from their agents. Why? Because three key factors kept them from knowing how much better things could be:

One, most people buy or sell a house only once every 10 or 15 years. That's the only time they work with a real estate agent, so they don't know what the service level should be. As a result, they're actually less picky about the service they receive from an agent handling a huge financial transaction than they are with, say, a hairdresser they see once a month.

Two, the phenomenon of "multi-generational real estate agents." A couple hires a young agent. Their kids and grandkids use the same one, and the agent eventually treats this as an excuse to offer subpar service. The customer doesn't know the difference.

And three, people often think they need a "neighborhood specialist" when they really need a marketing specialist. "Knowing the neighborhood" was a big advantage decades ago, before we entered the data-driven age. Today, any agent can get to know a neighborhood if they work hard enough. The bigger question is, can they generate demand for your property?

The key to providing superior customer service was always clear to me: Create a team that's ready to serve every customer. That's the only way to deliver the service that homebuyers and sellers deserve. And a team backed by a highly recognized brand gives agents an invaluable level of authority and trust. This increases their personal business and creates a true partnership that benefits both the customer and the agent.

I had employed freelancers almost from day one as an agent. As I accelerated my business growth, I needed a dedicated team to be as relentless as I was in delivering the most convenient experience in my market. If great photos were the best way to win the online beauty contest, I would bring in architectural photographers. If staging could make or break a home sale, I would hire stagers. Of course I needed agents, so I designed a system and team culture where agents could *support* each other rather than *compete against* each other.

Most importantly, I made the decision to build a personal brand and out-market everyone else. I noticed that when people buy or sell a house, they remember their agent's name, not their brokerage's name. It's "Jane Doe sold my house," not "ABC Realty sold my house." I decided to use that to our advantage in an aggressive way. In real estate, the more brand recognition you have, the more your customers benefit.

Enter the Kris Lindahl Team.

145

I chose to name the team after me because it created a more intimate customer experience. Putting my name, face and voice front and center certainly cut through the clutter. It also meant that the buck would *stop* with me and the leads would *start* with me. If you hired the Kris Lindahl Team, you might not get me as your actual agent, but you'd always get me (and my entire team) working on your behalf.

This strategy was the ultimate "high risk/high reward" approach, but I focused on the rewards. No one is great at everything, so we would put each team member in the right seat, doing what they do best. I would focus on my biggest strength — marketing — and my team could consistently over-deliver because of the collective experience and knowledge we had gained after working with so many homeowners and buyers.

Considering everything we brought to the table, customers were getting an absolute bargain. My agents could hit the ground running and focus on customer relationships instead of prospecting, and together we could build a convenience-based real estate operation that mirrored the success I saw in businesses like Amazon. Similar to Amazon, I was the name and face of the brand, but consumers were getting a team behind them. After all, when you buy something from Amazon, Jeff Bezos doesn't fulfill your order and deliver your package.

> *"When you buy or sell a house, you remember your agent's name, not their brokerage's name."*

Luckily for me, I now knew what did and didn't work in traditional real estate. Similar to the way I rose from sorting nightcrawlers to leading sales efforts at the pro shop in high school, I had already worn every hat in my industry. I knew the pain points and how to solve them. That breadth of experience also helped me in hiring, because agents respect you more when you've "been there, done that" in the business.

The Kris Lindahl Team grew like crazy. Then we moved to a different brokerage and became their largest team. Our secret sauce: Just like the most successful sports teams, we had the best locker room. We offered a better overall experience to consumers while also working behind the scenes to help each other.

Core Value: Owning It

The team concept works when each "player" knows their role and feels accountable for its success. That's what I built with the Kris Lindahl Team. It worked because an "own it" mentality always delivers a better customer experience.

Have you ever felt like you're wearing too many hats or you constantly have to do other people's jobs?

On the positive side, when have you worked in a true team environment where each player supported the other and you succeeded as a group?

17. 4 Benefits of "Team"

A FRIEND OF mine played tight end for the Indianapolis Colts when Peyton Manning and Tony Dungy led that team to the Super Bowl in 2007. My favorite story of his from those days centers on the concept of FAMILY: "Forget About Me, I Love You." Here's the gist of it:

Tony Dungy had brought the FAMILY mindset to the Colts after learning it from Chuck Noll and the Pittsburgh Steelers. A key part of FAMILY was "Family Saturdays," when the team would end practices early so the players' families could visit. Most of the players loved this tradition, but not Peyton Manning. Being young, single and an intense competitor, he saw Family Saturdays as a distraction — especially all those kids running around the field and in the locker rooms.

Years later, Manning had a family of his own and found himself playing for the Denver Broncos. Sensing that something was missing in the Broncos' team culture, he realized that building a better team off the field with the Colts had created a better team on the field. He walked up to Coach John Fox and exclaimed, "You know what we need here, Coach? Family Saturdays!"

Many industries fall short in creating healthy teams, and that's too bad. Because in my experience, achieving a positive team culture delivers four invaluable benefits:

1. An "Abundance Mindset"

I constantly make instructional videos for my agents with titles like "14 Steps to Growing Your Business." Most real estate team leaders don't do this because they don't want their teams to get "distracted" by focusing on their personal business. That's a "scarcity" mindset: *I'm not going to share because you might steal from me!*

Healthy teams have an abundance mindset. That's why thousands of entrepreneurs give their knowledge away for free on YouTube and social media. They don't worry about people "taking" what they know. They share it because it benefits everybody and builds loyalty. As a friend of mine likes to say, "The only thing worse than investing in someone and having them leave is not investing in them and having them stay."

2. Resilience

Things go wrong all the time. What matters is how you react when they do. Some people shut down because they've never learned how to process adversity. I often ask people to share a time when something went wrong in their life, and how they responded to it. Their answers tell me everything I need to know about them. One thing I've noticed: If you have a solid team sports background, then you're probably better at picking yourself up after adversity.

3. Accountability

Who can forget watching Reggie Miller score 8 points in 9 seconds to help the Pacers beat the Knicks in the 1995 NBA playoffs? (YouTube it.) Like elite athletes, successful real estate agents embrace accountability and perform best when their backs are against the wall. *But wait, wasn't Miller's accomplishment an individual effort?* No, it was a team leader taking accountability for his role. Who passed him the ball? What did the coach say during timeouts? The team knew he was their go-to guy, and he succeeded because of the coach and team around him.

"I often ask people to share a time when something went wrong in their life, and how they responded to it. Their answers tell me everything I need to know about them."

4. Positive Energy

We've all experienced teammates who make non-stop excuses. Nothing seems to go their way. They don't get the ball enough. The coach is against them. No one recognizes their talent. Hopefully, you've also played with positive team leaders or been one yourself. These are the people who say, "Here's how we're going to make this work and win." In sports, business and life, we "follow the leader." A leader who sets a positive tone lifts everybody up.

Bottom line: Teams can accomplish what individuals can't. If you want to go fast, go alone. But if you want to go far, go together. Unfortunately, as I was about to find out in my personal life, sometimes teams also break up.

Core Values: Staying Positive, Owning It

Teams are complex organisms. If you have a positive leader who instills accountability throughout the group, then the whole will exceed the individual parts, and you'll win championships. If negativity and entitlement take over, the opposite will happen.

Have you experienced a leader — in sports, business or life — who infused a positive and infectious spirit throughout the team? Have you also experienced the opposite?

What kind of leader are you, and how can you be a better one?

2,114 Mittens
& Lessons in Generosity

I experienced a life-changing event in January 2013. Actually, I instigated it by coming up with an idea that quickly grew out of control (big surprise). It proved to be a valuable lesson in the power of generosity and the importance of using your platform to help people.

The social media trend at that time was kids posting photos of themselves holding up signs like "Mom says if I get 1,000 likes, I can get a new bike!" I was fascinated by how quickly this craze took off. It sparked instant engagement because it made altruism easy: Click "Like" and make a child happy!

I loved the concept, but I wasn't crazy about the focus. What if I did something to help people who really needed it? I thought. I'd built a Facebook following of over 10,000 people, so I posted a photo of myself holding a sign promising that for every like, I would donate a pair of mittens to a local homeless shelter.

I expected a strong response, but I wasn't prepared for the avalanche that followed. The likes kept pouring in. A hundred pairs of mittens? I could do that. But 500? 750? 1,000? Uh-oh …

After just two hours, my mitten commitment far exceeded my budget. In the end, I bought and delivered over 2,000 pairs of mittens to seven different homeless shelters. The people who ran these facilities were as blown away as I was. "Who is this guy, and how is he able to give us all these mittens?"

I shared the process on social media because I wanted to inspire others and prove that I followed through on my promises. I also wanted to capture the moment for myself, because it was rewiring my brain in an interesting way. I had always believed in giving back. Now I saw what that could really look like, and how it could scale.

I also realized that a corporate real estate brokerage couldn't have inspired that kind of response. I could do it because I had built a personal brand with thousands of social media followers. I was humbled to see the full potential of our connection, and I knew that I was doing the right thing.

A few years later, my friend Darin Dawson invited me to fly to Colorado Springs and speak to his employees at BombBomb, the highly successful video, email and text company. Once I got there, I immediately saw another unique opportunity to focus a group's energy on a good cause.

BombBomb's mission is "to rehumanize the planet." They were heavily involved with a nonprofit that helped impoverished residents of a rural Kenyan community called Mount Elgon CarePoint, and the goal was helping people achieve sustainability through farming and infrastructure. I loved that idea. So when I took the stage, I presented a challenge: "If you donate to that nonprofit right now, I'll match your donation up to $5,000."

People had expected me to share my knowledge of

marketing, branding and entrepreneurship at the event. I gave them that, but I also used a portion of my time to create awareness for something bigger — a cause that also perfectly fit their mission.

We raised a lot of money that day, and we experienced a collective feeling of power, openness, warmth and welcoming. To show my gratitude, I gave everyone who donated a Be Generous T-shirt, which continued to spread that important message. Everyone felt good that they had worked together to help people half a world away, and we knew we had accomplished something as a team that we could never have done as individuals. I'll never forget it.

18. Divorce Hits Home

Rachel and I married in 2010, and by 2017 our beautiful daughter, Victoria ("V"), was 8 years old. On one hand, pouring myself into work had given V a stability I never knew. Ironically, it also masked some of the same marital problems I advised my clients to solve before selling their properties.

I was surrounded by unhealthy relationships growing up, especially my parents'. I'd never had a role model for being a spouse. All I knew was how to work, so I focused on outworking everyone around me. That brought me success in sports and business, but it didn't help my marriage. Like so many couples, Rachel and I gradually became friends and roommates. We could still be a strong team for our daughter, but we weren't meant to be married, and my work obsession only delayed that realization.

I'm fortunate that our divorce was, and continues to be, an amicable one. I can't imagine a better mother for our daughter than Rachel. I've seen so many relationships end in bitterness, with kids stuck in the center of a toxic tug-of-war that damages them for life. People on the outside don't believe me when I say that Rachel and I don't have any real conflicts. But anyone who knows us understands. She even surprised me years ago by putting up a billboard featuring V doing the "Arms Out" pose and wishing me a happy Father's Day. I'm still touched by that.

Our divorce did, however, open up some internal wounds. I was 8 when my parents announced their split. Victoria was now even younger than that. Divorce is never easy for a child, but Rachel and I wanted to protect Victoria from its worst effects. We never used the word "divorce" around her. We told her that we were no longer going to be together, but we framed it in a constructive way. We maintain that positive attitude to this day, never bad-mouthing each other and always putting her interests first.

For me, that started with housing. Being forced to leave my house due to my parents' split had left a deep scar. Life had felt good and stable, then my house, neighborhood and friends were gone in a flash. I didn't want that for Victoria, so I made sure that she and Rachel could stay in the only home Victoria knew.

On a personal level, I couldn't shake the thought that I had failed at something big. Up to that point, I was convinced that I could control my destiny if I always worked harder and thought smarter. How did I get my marriage so wrong? How could I have believed so much in "growth" and "development" while also having such a huge blind spot?

I wanted to be the best dad possible, so I bought a boat that Victoria and I could take trips on, the water providing the perfect environment for us to talk. Other times, I would go solo and reflect on my life to that point. I let it sink in that despite my professional successes, my most important

Want to live a more Arms Out life? You're not alone! Use the QR code below to register for our FREE newsletter. It's a great way to take your inspiration to the next level.

relationship had failed. Teachers and coaches had taught me so many life lessons, but not how to communicate with a spouse. To make matters worse, my career had put me in front of dysfunctional couples nearly every day. Maybe that's all I knew because that's all I saw.

Any failed relationship has plenty of blame to go around, but the only person I could change was me. I had to face a hard fact: I thought I was an engaged spouse, but I had actually been missing in action in many ways. I couldn't let that happen again, so I dug deep to figure out the kind of relationship I really wanted. I didn't want to stay with someone who wasn't the right fit just because it was "the right thing to do," as some of the older people I knew did. I also didn't want to be a "player" and live a superficial, uncommitted life like other single men my age. Change comes from within, so I needed to find a better mindset.

I wrote down two phrases during this time: "Be Still" and "Be Present." I had to stop bouncing all over the place, being on my phone constantly and living in a state of distraction. I worked hard to slow down — not to stop moving, but to be in the moment instead of always someplace else. That's hard for restless types like me. Visionaries are wired to *anticipate*, and you get rewarded for it. Unfortunately, it leads to a contradictory feeling that successful entrepreneurs know well:

The root of your success in one area is the root of your failure in another, because you're always looking around the next corner.

I'm still a work in progress, but the older I get, the more I want to stay present. Today, I've never been more grateful for simple conversations with friends. I don't care how often we agree or disagree. It's about being together, but it's also about saying, "Hey, I just want to let you know how much I appreciate our friendship. Thank you."

I've lost significant people in my life, and I know how it feels to regret the things you didn't say and the feelings you never expressed. I'm still learning how *not* to get lost in the past or distracted by the future. My goal is simple: Every night before I go to bed, I want to be able to say to myself, "Today, I paid attention, I listened, I gave everything I had, and I appreciated everything life had to offer."

"I've lost significant people in my life, and I know how it feels to regret the things you didn't say and the feelings you never expressed."

I'm lucky to have a partner who helps me do that. Gina and I fell for each other instantly in 2017, and we've been together ever since. She knows my "good, bad and ugly," and she keeps me grounded when my brain gets too excited — which is often. (Frankly, she would describe it as a full-time job.) Our chemistry allows us to make each other better while also remaining 100% ourselves. That's something I never saw in romantic relationships when I was growing up, and I couldn't be more grateful to Gina for showing me how it's possible.

Gina has also given me the wonderful gift of her daughter, Gianna. As I write this, Gianna is navigating college, trying out new things and going through that critical process of figuring out who you are and what you want to be. I love playing a role in helping her discover her best self, and I'm so excited to see where she takes her life.

Speaking of figuring out who you are and being your authentic self, at this point in my career I was about to launch a new marketing campaign that felt more "me" than anything I'd ever done before. My hope was that it would help my business. It ended up changing my life.

Core Value: Owning It

My divorce made me realize that I'd never had a "relationship mentor," but it also forced me to own up to the fact that I hadn't been fully present as a partner. Going through that process has allowed me to slow down and better prioritize my life.

Have you ever thought you were fully present in a relationship, then realized later that you weren't? How did you change?

Do you have a mentor or role model when it comes to relationships? How have they helped you in your personal life?

ARMS OUT

19. The Photo

ONE SPRING DAY in 2017, I woke up with my mind bouncing all over the place. I'd spent the previous day playing catch-up after a vacation, and I was in "disorganized visionary" mode when a panicked thought hit me:

I have a photo shoot this morning!

After years of focusing on social media and other marketing tactics, I was now buying outdoor advertising for the first time. My creative agency said it was time to change my billboards, and they had scheduled a photo shoot. Not wanting to be late, I grabbed whatever clothes I could find and headed out without bothering to shave.

I dreaded photo shoots — the forced smiles, the weight of carrying all the shirts, pants, belts, suit coats, shoes and hangers. My previous billboard had featured me in nine different outfits because the Kris Lindahl Team was selling a house every nine hours. I expected the same type of shoot that day, which is why I'd brought so many clothes. But as I stood against a white background striking different poses in different outfits, nothing felt right. I wanted to differentiate myself and my team from all the smiling agents in their perfectly pressed suits, but how?

I don't remember exactly what led me to throw my arms out, but I do remember it feeling liberating. Especially without a jacket on, the gesture was energetic, spontaneous and authentic. I did as many "Arms Out" shots as I could before my arms nearly fell off.

Days after the shoot, I had over 30 photos to choose from. The one I picked has appeared in most of my advertising ever since — billboards, digital ads, yard signs, buses, trains, TV commercials, airplane banners and everywhere else. Based on the dozens of parody versions that people have made (and continue to make) of that image, it's safe to say that it's made a lasting impression.

The Arms Out pose works because it matches my personality. It's emotional. It draws you in with a big "yes" that suggests community, generosity and positivity. And it's different from what real estate agents and brokerages normally do. No jacket. No tie. Just a tan, unshaven, smiling dude who looks like he wants to give you a great big hug. (For those who know the photo well, I'll clear some things up by revealing that while my teeth are slightly whitened, the tan and stubble are real. Also, the reason my ring and pinky fingers almost touch on my left hand is because I broke that pinky so many times playing football.)

The Arms Out pose works because it matches my personality. It's emotional. It draws you in with a big 'yes' that suggests community, generosity and positivity.

Today, my Arms Out image is iconic in my markets and beyond. People have Photoshopped it onto "Game of Thrones" posters and Land O'Lakes butter packages. It's been turned into Halloween costumes for adults, kids and even dogs. Activision, the video game developer now owned by Microsoft, even licensed it to help promote a new release of Call of Duty.

I knew I was cutting through the clutter when someone Photoshopped my billboard onto the surface of Mars and joked that it was the first photo taken by NASA's Perseverance rover. I'll never forget the moment when thousands of kids flung their arms out after seeing my image flash on the scoreboard during a Minnesota Wild hockey game. And Minnesota Twins fans are familiar with "stretching their arms like Kris Lindahl" during the 7th-inning stretch at home games.

My Arms Out image has now earned hundreds of millions of gross impressions and been seen by tens of millions of people. The fact that it has worked so well and become so big is no accident. It's the result of years and years of executing a strategic marketing and branding plan. Companies buy billboards all the time, and most consumers never notice them. Ours work because they didn't come out of nowhere. We only started using them after doing other things (print, social media, etc.) to build name and brand recognition. Now we have a first-mover advantage, so anyone who tries to copy our branding strategy only ends up helping us.

Not surprisingly, the Arms Out image has also generated its share of criticism along the way. Anytime you put yourself out there and build a personal brand — especially as consistently as I have — you inspire a backlash. People will say they're sick of seeing you. They'll call you a narcissist. And, as I mentioned earlier in this book, they'll even fabricate rumors about your personal life to knock you down a peg.

They'll also copy you, which moved me in 2022 to register the Arms Out symbol as a trademark for our real estate and related services. Our goal was simple: We had to protect our brand on behalf of our team and our clients. The intent was never about trying to stop the general public from holding their arms out or doing the pose. I love that! But — as the Call of Duty licensing would soon reinforce — we had to recognize that the Arms Out image had become an iconic and valuable piece of intellectual property that helped our clients, and that it was uniquely associated with our brand.

But here's the interesting thing: When I eventually replaced the Arms Out image with an illustrated version of myself, the move generated a backlash to the backlash. I made the change knowing that I was doing my own version of the New Coke Effect, where taking a new spin on an established product makes people nostalgic for the original. Sure enough, as soon as the illustrated image appeared, people wanted Classic Kris back. I fueled the "controversy" by creating a Facebook poll where I asked people to vote on which billboard they preferred. The original Arms Out image won by a margin of about 98% to 2%. It may have been the first time in history that people actively *wanted* a billboard.

I used to make fun of real estate agents who kept the same business card headshot for 20 years; now I'm doing the same thing on a massive scale, because that 2017 image remains central to my brand. It has even helped me reinvent the yard sign. During the pandemic, we decided to make my signs stand out by changing them to Arms Out cutouts instead of the standard rectangle. When sign materials were hard to find, we cleaned out inventories at Lowe's and Home Depot. When sign companies said they didn't know how to install a custom sign, we started our own sign company.

What's that word again? Oh yeah, "tenacity"! It was a lot of work, but it paid off. Our yard signs now work a lot harder to sell homes. Instead of promoting an individual real estate agent, they drive demand among buyers because they reinforce the most recognizable name, image and team in our markets. In effect, every homeowner who works with us gets the benefit of hundreds of additional billboards.

Back in 2017, my entire marketing campaign — including the new billboards — attracted so many leads that a new thought began to nag at me: *What if I started my own brokerage?* I assumed I would act on that vision in two or three years. Fate had a shorter timeline in mind.

———

Core Values: Tenacity, Staying Positive

I was always a tenacious marketer eager to try new things. Once I found an image that helped build my personal brand and felt authentic to my positive energy, my business took off like never before.

What's your personal brand? Is it innovative, high-energy and welcoming like mine, or is it more thoughtful, private and subdued?

There's no "right" personality for a personal brand. How can you find one that feels authentic and sustainable?

20. Changing the Game

AT THIS POINT in my career, I already knew what it was like to face difficult life situations. I had also sat across the kitchen table from thousands of people dealing with divorce, job loss, financial hardship, impending foreclosure, a death in the family, you name it.

I soon realized that so many people dealing with these hard situations needed a better way to navigate them. Shouldn't their property be an asset that helps them instead of a liability that hurts them? Shouldn't their property help to lower their risk instead of raising it? At the same time, I saw so many others trying to sell properties that needed tens of thousands of dollars in repairs and renovations — money they simply didn't have. So they felt stuck.

In short, I realized people needed something that the

current real estate market simply wasn't offering them:

- A way to get fair and competitive offers on their house

- A fast, simple and convenient process for selling it

- A trustworthy and compassionate team to listen and offer them real solutions instead of judging or taking advantage of them

- Relief from feeling stuck and overwhelmed

- An easier and more reliable way to get where they want to go and be who they want to be

"Acquisition companies" already existed — those often faceless cash homebuyers with a reputation for ignoring, lowballing, insulting and abandoning homeowners. But I didn't see them as a good option for people. So in 2017, I decided to build on the foundation of trust we'd already created and launch something that would shake up the market and meet a massive consumer need. I called it the *Guaranteed Cash Offer*.

A *Guaranteed Cash Offer* would help multiple kinds of homeowners: the ones facing adversity and the ones who appreciated the value of time and convenience. The concept was simple: We already trade in our cars "as is"; why not our properties? As a homeowner, you would get a competitive cash offer (not an insulting lowball) on your house *fast*, based on its location, condition and other market factors. If you accepted it, you would get the money quickly, without paying a penny in commissions or closing costs. Then you could choose your closing date — soon if you valued speed or months away if that worked better for you.

Guaranteed Cash Offer was more than a program; it posed some big, provocative questions: Why did selling a house have to be such a stressful experience, and why didn't a better option exist for selling a property for cash? Industries like shopping, technology and transportation had already been disrupted and improved by companies who found ways to better meet evolving consumer needs. What about real estate?

The enthusiastic response to *Guaranteed Cash Offer* validated my thinking: For a growing number of homeowners, the traditional "open market" system for selling a house no longer fit their needs. They didn't like losing their privacy by publicly listing their house. They didn't like spending crazy amounts of time and money on repairs, renovations, showings and open houses. They were losing days of sleep, living every day feeling anxious and uncertain, only to end up losing up to 10% of their home sale to commissions and closing costs. They wanted a fresh new option, and now they had it.

Based on where *Guaranteed Cash Offer* is today, it's safe to say I was onto something. The program has taken the country by storm, grown like crazy and inspired many (pale) imitations from coast to coast.

Today, urban, suburban and rural homeowners have learned the advantages of accepting a *Guaranteed Cash Offer*. It's helped people facing financial challenges, relocating for work, dealing with an aging relative's house as they transition to senior living and so many other situations. It's an option for *anyone* who worries about economic uncertainty and wants to avoid exposing their house to a potentially risky, slow-moving and constantly changing open market.

Our program continues to be the industry pioneer, now offering people additional convenience options around packing, decluttering and moving. I had the advantage of being a "first mover," but I think *Guaranteed Cash Offer* remains the clear leader because it comes from a place of empathy. As you've now seen, I grew up in a financially challenged household where we were forced to move constantly. I learned to value "home" at an early age. I also benefited from teachers, coaches and other mentors who believed in me and gave me a helping hand. That's why I'm more passionate than ever about helping people sell their properties with speed, convenience and dignity so they can move on to the next chapter of their lives.

Core Values: Tenacity, Empathy, Generosity

From both my difficult upbringing and my experience as a real estate agent, I learned that many people need help facing challenging life situations that involve their house. Many others simply want a faster and more convenient way to sell their property. This option didn't exist, so I created it myself with the *Guaranteed Cash Offer* program.

What's an industry you think needs a dose of reform and innovation?

Do you find yourself coming up with your own ideas on how to improve the way businesses operate?

21. A Company Is Born Overnight

BY THE SPRING of 2018, the Kris Lindahl Team had become one of the biggest real estate teams at one of the country's largest brokerages. We had our own offices and did our own branding and marketing. Our operation was self-contained and self-sustaining.

When a smaller group within a larger structure achieves a certain level of success, conflicts tend to emerge. That's exactly what happened between us and our brokerage. They thought they deserved a bigger share of our huge business volume. From my perspective, we were succeeding as the Kris Lindahl Team, and the systems and branding we'd built ourselves had minimized the brokerage's value.

The inevitable happened at the end of May, when we mutually agreed to part ways within 30 days. I shook their

© 2025 KL Brands, LLC

hands, told them I appreciated the opportunity they had given me, and wished them good luck. The next day, I was told that I only had until the following Thursday to set up my own shop. Monday was Memorial Day, so that meant four business days to legally launch a new brand and brokerage.

Crises require fast and open communication. So before I had time to organize my thoughts, I invited my entire team to a Facebook Live. Many of them showed up with their spouses and kids, which was a profound reminder of how high the stakes were on my next move. *Make no mistake*, the images of families on my screen told me, *your decisions are about to affect more than your business.*

"Our time here is going to be short, and we have to turn a lot of things around fast," I said. "I'm starting Kris Lindahl Real Estate, and we're going to continue our success." I explained the situation in as much detail as I could and told everyone I was absolutely confident we would make the transition in time.

I read the concern on people's faces, but I didn't feel panicked; I felt energized. I feed on adversity and have a way of finding clarity in chaos. I wasn't just *saying* that things would work out for the best. I *believed* it. But I'm still human. After I closed my screen, my first thought was *How on earth are you going to pull this off?*

I had already taken the most important step: engaging in open, honest and timely communication. The brokerage failed to recruit my people away from me a few days later because my team had heard from me first and liked my message better.

I kept my team, but I faced a different challenge. A legal

one. I had a broker's license. Now I learned that you have to apply for both a brokerage and an entity, and this normally takes several weeks. Without that license, my team would fall into legal limbo and our pending transactions would disappear. My team wouldn't be able to follow me, because as far as the government was concerned, I wouldn't exist.

I filled out the necessary paperwork and drove it to the State Capitol in St. Paul myself. I assumed that I'd be able to talk to someone at the state licensing office and maybe pay an "expedited process" fee. No dice.

Bandwidth on the governmental side was proving to be a problem. I understood why no one cared about a business dispute between a real estate brokerage and one of its former team leaders, but I saw a bigger issue: Hundreds of homeowners and buyers in the state were about to be displaced through no fault of their own. If your job is to protect consumers, my argument went, then you should care about this.

While I scrambled to find a solution to the license problem, the rumor mill churned up and calls from reporters flooded my phone.

"I heard you were kicked out of your brokerage and are in trouble with compliance. Any comment?" was a typical question. *What?* I had to change our entire brand identity to Kris Lindahl Real Estate overnight, and now I had to spend precious hours correcting misinformation?

Thanks to our big brand and its potential effects on the people who counted on us — and through the incredible efforts of my internal and external teams (you know who you are, but I'll call out Kat, Meghan and Tracy) — the Kris Lindahl Real Estate brand came into being just four days after the brokerage and I had parted ways. We had a new logo, new lawn signs on order and new digital billboards in place. We executed an entire corporate rebrand in 48 hours, which must be a record.

The best part is, most people didn't even notice. We were already strongly branded as the Kris Lindahl Team. To the average person, the only difference was the appearance of a Kris Lindahl Real Estate logo. That's when I realized that our *real* logo was the Arms Out image. It represented who we were and what we stood for better than our corporate logo ever could. It was our Nike swoosh.

Finally, on the Wednesday after Memorial Day — one day before my team would have lost everything we had built — the state approved my application. The last puzzle piece snapped into place. And a new company was officially born.

That's when I realized that our real logo was the Arms Out image. It represented who we were and what we stood for better than our corporate logo ever could.

Life delivers moments that can feel like mortal blows. This one didn't compare to my parents' separation, losing the family home, trying to break up a gunfight or learning about my father's death. But launching a new company in one week proved to be the most relentless and amazing team effort I'd ever been a part of. Was it a huge accomplishment? Yes, and I hope I never have to do it again.

It was also the first step on a much bigger journey. Now that I had taken total control of my team, a new question entered my mind: *How are we going to keep changing things for the better?* I had some ideas ...

Core Values: Tenacity, Staying Positive, Owning It

The way my team parted ways with my former brokerage put me in a Houdini-like situation. Somehow I had to unlock the chains, slip out of the straitjacket and emerge from the water in less a week. I did it by owning the situation, staying positive, communicating openly and honestly with my team, and doing everything possible to get my new company legally operating.

What's the biggest curveball life has ever thrown you, and how did you handle it? Do crises energize you or make you panic?

When has another leader helped you — or failed to help you — navigate a tough situation?

ARMS
OUT

22. A Fresh Approach

AFTER I LAUNCHED my company, people started treating me differently. When I was a team leader at a big brokerage, I was a real estate agent. Now that I owned my own business, I was an entrepreneur.

With a jolt of new confidence, I saw unlimited possibilities. My team and I could do anything we wanted, so we put our heads together and decided to go full "Frank Sinatra": From our business model and marketing to our internal culture and community involvement, we would do it our way. Here's how:

183

Structure

Most traditional brokerages are bound to a master franchise in another state. The local franchises have limited power, and they rely on their individual agents to generate business by connecting with their friends and family. In essence, the agents take on all the risk and generate most of the business. That's why real estate agents spend so much of their time prospecting: They're the salespeople on the front lines, and they're on their own.

We would have a CEO (me) with full control over the company. We already had a powerful brand that people wanted to work with. Now we could double and triple the strength of our reach and frequency. By creating an enhanced "big brand" structure, our agents could receive a steady stream of warm leads and focus on what they were most passionate about: helping people. As a bonus, our agents' friends and family proactively reached out to them because they trusted our brand, creating a winning combo. And the cherry on top: Our local presence helped us achieve economies of scale that out-of-state parent brands couldn't match.

To this day, 90% of our business comes directly through our branding, which frees our agents to focus on the customer experience. Speaking of which …

The Customer Experience

Once we achieved brand equity as the "Kris Lindahl Team," we needed to protect what we had built. Most importantly, we had to take total ownership of the consumer experience. As a team within a big brokerage model, we couldn't do that. As our own company, we could. This point is worth a deeper dive, because most people don't understand how traditional brokerages work.

In the conventional real estate model, when you hire your friend who's an agent at Big Traditional Brokerage (BTB), BTB has no visibility into the level of service your friend delivers. Maybe she's great, maybe you haven't heard from her in weeks. BTB doesn't know, and they wouldn't know what to do about it even if they *did* know.

In our brand- and customer-centric team model, we would 100% own the customer experience. The relationship would start with us (due to our strong brand), then move to the agents. But we would maintain visibility into the level of customer service our agents delivered. We'd make sure they talked to customers often, and we'd know if they didn't. We would also improve the experience of our other key customers by improving ...

The Agent Experience

Our model provided strength in areas where traditional agents are usually deficient — something I understood because I had worn every hat along the way. For example, most brokerages claim to have brands, but they basically use their agents to give them a small amount of advertising through For Sale signs in yards. To really succeed, agents need to build a brand that consumers trust. Doing that involves a level of risk that most either can't or don't want to take on.

As stated earlier, we would "de-risk" real estate for agents by taking care of the most expensive and time-consuming part of their jobs: getting customers. Our brand was already strong and would keep getting stronger through our aggressive marketing. By giving agents leads instead of expecting them to constantly mine them, we would improve their experience by covering so many of the things they don't want to do, freeing them to focus on customer service.

Another issue with agents in traditional brokerages is that they're isolated and on their own, often glued to their job without support. We would offer a team culture of generosity where others will cover so an agent can take time off and achieve the right work-life balance.

Our agents wouldn't have to feel like no one had their back.

If we wanted our internal culture to appeal to agents, we would have to place a strong emphasis on …

Communication

I saw a need for clearer, more centralized communication at my traditional brokerages — both inside the company and with customers. Brokerages have almost no control over the quality and quantity of customer contact because it passes through their individual agents. The brokerage depends on those agents to be effective communicators, but most aren't because they've never been trained.

Internal communication lacks even more in the traditional model. When I was an agent in that system, I never felt connected to the parent brand. Communication should have been a constant dialogue about how to improve the customer experience. Instead, it felt irregular, disjointed and one-sided.

As with our marketing and customer service, we would place our company brand at the center of communication. We would have direct conversations with our agents and customers. We would invest in technology to improve communication. And we would create a consistent dialogue so agents and customers would always feel heard. That would fit our personality because it would fit our ...

Culture & Values

Buying and selling houses is a great way to make a living, but it pales in comparison to connecting with people and standing for something bigger. When your job is tied to a mission, you never want to hit the snooze button. Work doesn't feel like work, because you're making the world a better place and leaving the campground better than you found it.

Within a traditional, big-brokerage structure, it's hard to feel like you're contributing to the greater good — especially when national franchisees suck their profits out of the community and out of state. Remembering how I felt coaching youth basketball, giving away those mittens and participating in other community events throughout my life, I had an epiphany: The feeling I get from sports and connecting with people is nothing compared to the feeling I get from giving back.

I wanted to capture that feeling with my company. We didn't have the large franchise fees coming off the top, so we could give back locally and invest more back into the customer journey. We could also stand for something bigger in the world, which is how we ended up with the core values I shared at the beginning of this book: Learning, Empathy, Tenacity, Staying Positive, Generosity and Owning It, spelling out our rally cry "LET'S GO!"

My favorite part of our core values is our passion for giving back to our ...

Community

Big, slow-moving real estate brokerages can't holistically serve the communities where they do business. They aren't nimble enough to organize an event next week for their clients or head to Feed My Starving Children tomorrow to pack food for families in need. For the most part, it's the individual agents who have to decide if and how they want to help their communities.

The Kris Lindahl Team had already mobilized several times to serve our neighbors. Our best example was creating the Great Pumpkin Giveaway in 2014, which grew from a small giveaway to a massive event with food and entertainment. We even set a Guinness World Record in 2016 for the longest line of continuous pumpkins: 8,672 zigzagging for nearly a mile.

Kris Lindahl Real Estate vowed to do even more, and in 2020, the coronavirus pandemic provided our biggest opportunity. While traditional brokerages struggled to find their footing, our centralized structure freed us to move our energy wherever it was needed most. During another unrehearsed fireside video chat, I told my team: "Look, I don't know what's going to happen with this pandemic, but we're going to get through it. Right now, it's about people, not business. We're moving our marketing budget into helping people, so let's talk about what we can do."

Ideas poured out. We hired out-of-work Uber drivers to deliver groceries to people in need. We engaged people on social media to tell us which small businesses they cared about, then bought hundreds of gift cards to support them. We changed our billboards to promote "humanity over business." And we launched a first-of-its-kind scholarship program to help more people afford their real estate licenses. Today, tens of thousands of people have applied for a Kris Lindahl Real Estate Scholarship, and some have become our best agents.

And here's my favorite story: After we asked the people in our network if they needed help, we heard from a woman in her 80s. Katherine was a past client who lived alone in a high-rise. She was terrified to leave her condo. She didn't have family nearby. And she didn't know how to use Instacart, Shipt or any other delivery service. We were the only people she could talk to, because we were the only ones who had reached out. We found out what she needed, and we stocked her condo with groceries and other supplies.

Did our business suffer because we got "distracted" by helping people like Katherine during the worst days of the pandemic? No, it grew. We became the #1 independent brokerage in our state. And in 2022, "Real Trends" ranked us as America's 5th largest "mega team," with over 4,400 transactions and nearly $1.4 billion in closed sales. I realized that "Arms Out" was a lot more than a pose. It was a mindset, a way of life and an idea worth sharing.

Core Values: All of Them

When I started my own company, I was free to do things my own way. When I translated my personal core values into corporate ones, our team felt energized, our customers and communities benefited, and our business took off. We continue to foster a culture of Learning, Empathy, Tenacity, Staying Positive, Generosity and Owning It: *LET'S GO!*

What are your core values? Have you ever taken the time to list them?

How do you apply your personal core values to your professional life?

Have you experienced the difference between working with a company that knows and lives its core values vs. one that doesn't?

Especially after everything that's happened over the last several years, have you revisited your core values to make sure they're still the right ones?

Always Learning (People)

In addition to educating myself through books, programs and events, I'm fortunate to have a core group of friends and colleagues. Here's a few I'd like to thank:

Real estate mega-coach Jon Cheplak (Cheplak Live) provides a great example of leadership and has taught me the importance of resilience. The path he chose (and continues to choose) in dealing with his alcoholism gives me the "happy ending" version that my dad's life lacked. I'm so grateful for the energy and expertise he poured into our company, especially as we were just starting out. He's been an incredible mentor and a great friend. And I was happy to return the favor by telling him that he had something special to offer and should reach more people with it. Thank you, Jon.

Gary Ashton (The Gary Ashton Team) is a big personality who constantly teaches me the importance of "owning it." He moved to the U.S. from England without much of anything and continues to dominate the Nashville market, and he was miles ahead of the industry when it comes to SEO, web development and owning data. Thank you, Gary.

Canadian superstar Justin Havre (Justin Havre Real Estate Team) is another great example of grit and resilience. He moved to Canada from Norway without knowing the language or having a community, and now he's the dominant real estate entrepreneur in Calgary. Thank you, Justin.

Event production visionary Charles Eide (EideCom) constantly teaches me the value of personal connection and helping others. We met at a charity event, and he constantly reinforces the importance of being generous. Thank you, Charles.

BombBomb co-founder Darin Dawson reinforces trust and integrity in my life every day. His loyalty, honesty and integrity are off the charts, and he always does what he says he's going to do. Thank you, Darin.

Outdoorsman and entrepreneur Tony Capra has increased my fishing prowess — and my business acumen — tenfold. Whether I'm hunting for fish, customers or other new innovations, he's taught me to be both aggressive and patient, to know where your opportunities lie, and to adapt to your conditions. Thank you, Tony.

I don't think there's anyone who has directly taught me more than high-performance trainer Brendon Burchard. Attending his High Performance Academy in 2015 changed my life by introducing me to the world of high-level personal development, improving my communication skills, and inspiring me to become a better leader and person. Thank you, Brendon.

Finally, my Kris Lindahl Real Estate colleagues and teammates. Not a day goes by that I don't learn valuable lessons on work and life from you. We truly are a team — one that has the best locker room and leaves it all on the field. It's been an incredible journey so far, and I couldn't be more excited to see where we go tomorrow. Thank you!

23. Arms Out

DESPERATE TO ESCAPE a bleak existence in the depths of a dark Northern Minnesota winter, I vowed at the age of 12 to take full ownership of my life. I've carried that sense of personal responsibility into adulthood, but make no mistake: My achievements are the result of a team effort.

I owe a huge debt of gratitude to dozens of generous people who have helped me throughout my life — the coaches, teachers, mentors, family members and friends who have recognized my hardships and understood my desire to create something better for myself and others. They've given me an internal voice that constantly taps me on the shoulder and asks, "Who can you help today?"

As a kid, I learned how much someone's words and actions can affect you in both positive and negative ways. As an adult, I have a simple mantra to positively impact everyone I come into contact with. My favorite moments are the surprises: hearing how much your words end up helping someone else, sometimes many years later.

On a small scale, I'll encourage entrepreneurs no matter how young they are. If I drive by a lemonade stand, I'll stop the car to buy a cup or two, talk to the kids like they're the next world-class entrepreneur, then leave them a big tip. (I have some really cute thank-you notes from many of them, likely written with a parent or two looking over their shoulder.)

I'll also offer advice to new and emerging entrepreneurs whenever I can. There's nothing magic about it. All I do is help them gain the confidence to realize their own visions. But I have to admit, nothing is more gratifying than hearing back from them about their successes. Some recent examples: A high school friend recently let me know that he took my advice from years ago and started a company that now employs over 300 people. A young entrepreneur I spoke to in 2017 recently sent me a message telling me that the food and beverage company I encouraged him to start was now earning millions in revenue. And my friend Charles Eide recently thanked me for talking him off the ledge during the Covid pandemic. Thanks to his vision and persistence, his event production and creative services company, EideCom, is doing better than ever.

As for my own ventures, do I take pride in what Kris Lindahl Real Estate has accomplished and the thousands of families we've helped? Absolutely. But more importantly, I'm proud of the ways our team continues to live an "Arms Out" life: Doing a $5,000 company match for a local homeless shelter. Donating 90 beds to My Very Own Bed, which makes sure that kids can sleep every night in their own bed. Buying new band instruments for a family who lost everything in a fire. Giving away a billboard to a kids' radio program in St. Paul. Helping raise over $40,000 for the family of a beloved youth hockey coach who died suddenly. Resurrecting WNBA legend Maya Moore's "Wings" billboard for Nike that inspired so many young women and girls like my daughter. And so much more.

"Life is full of challenges. Embrace them. You might be afraid to put yourself out there and be judged and criticized. Do it anyway."

In my speaking career, I've learned that sharing my story gives others a sense of hope. I feel it when I talk to students, real estate professionals, entrepreneurs, the general public and my own team. Whether I address kids or adults, small mastermind groups or large conventions, people hug me, take selfies with me and send me text messages about what inspires them. Each interaction is unique, but they're always about people seeing their struggles in mine and feeling a renewed strength to overcome them.

To those people, to the ones who have given *me* that

strength over the years, and to those of you who've taken the time to read my story in these pages, thank you. You mean the world to me.

To the younger people out there, I'll leave you with this:

Life is full of challenges. Embrace them. You might be afraid to put yourself out there and be judged and criticized. *Do it anyway*. Remember that what people say reveals more about *them* than you, and the opposite of love isn't hate; it's indifference. Millions of people love teams like the Yankees and Patriots, and millions more hate them, but no one is indifferent to them. When you represent a legacy of success, everybody *cares*. Even the haters know that the sports they love are better when they include the teams they root against.

I learned a long time ago that I can't control what anyone thinks about me. People will hold different opinions based on their own challenges and how well they actually know me. But I can honestly say that I want *everyone* to succeed. I hope my investments create a rising tide that lifts real estate and other industries, and I encourage other entrepreneurs around the world to apply their passions to shake things up and make the world a better place.

I call this "Living Life Arms Out." Life isn't a cutthroat, zero-sum game. There are millions of ways to grow and help others, and plenty of opportunities exist for everyone. This is what the Arms Out gesture ultimately means. I encourage you to strike the pose yourself, share it on social media and tag me. The more people who live life Arms Out, the better off we'll all be.

My advice for the entrepreneurs of tomorrow: Focus on

you and *your* mission. Don't be afraid. Don't retreat. Don't close yourself off. Don't disappear. Look every challenge in the eyes. Let a big smile spread across your face. And stretch your arms out as far as they can go.

Searching for More?

Let's talk!

So many people want a career that offers purpose, meaning and unlimited growth. Our unique application process identifies A players who want to go to the next level. If you're one of them, introduce yourself!

Go to **KrisLindahl.com/now-hiring**
or scan the QR code below.

Epilogue

AN EXPERIENCE WITH my (now teenage) daughter, Victoria, strikes me as a good way to end this book. Gina and I had planned a family trip to Florida. We told Victoria that she could take someone along, and she chose her friend "Amanda."

I had noticed a few things about Amanda — mostly that she seemed to really like our home and was often reluctant to leave. Then when we picked her up, I noticed that she was hauling a familiar-looking suitcase.

"Look at that, V, Amanda has the same suitcase as you!" I said.

"Dad, that *is* my suitcase," she replied. "I gave it to her because she's never taken a trip, so she doesn't have one."

I can't tell you how many memories of my own childhood came flooding back in that moment. The isolation. The stigma of not living in a traditional single-family home. The financial struggles. The parental fights. I thought about it on the drive to the airport and during the entire trip, but I kept it to myself.

After we flew back and dropped Amanda off, I finally spoke to V.

"I really like what you did with Amanda," I said.

"What do you mean?"

"Giving her your suitcase. That stuff is really important. Twenty-five years ago, that could have been me. I grew up like Amanda, and you remember the people who help you instead of judging you. You need to stay close to people like her."

"I know," she said in that *I get it, Dad, we don't need to dwell on this!* way. But I could see the wheels turning in her head.

Fast-forward a few weeks, and I'm picking V up early at school on a Friday. She's never asked for a day off before, and I don't love the idea, but I've decided to allow it just this once. When she gets in the car, she seems different. She asks me how my business is doing, which she's never done before. I give her the lowdown. Inventories are low, interest rates are volatile, the economy is shifting, but demand for our brand continues to grow, and we'll adapt and stay ahead of it like we always do.

She's pensive. This leads to me talking about how lucky we are, how other people are really struggling right now, and how it's always important to help out and give back.

"You're growing up in a much more stable and comfortable environment than I did, which is great," I say. "But it can create its own challenges in terms of motivation later on."

"I know," she says. "I see it all the time on social media. The most successful people are always the ones who had a tough time growing up. How old were you when your dad died?" she asks. I'm surprised at this twist, but I go with it. We're already an hour into what's normally a 20-minute drive, and I know we won't have these moments forever (she's driving now).

"I was 16."

"And your siblings?"

"Jamie was 14, Kory was 12."

"I'm 13," she says. She goes quiet. I can feel things clicking for her.

"Let's get some ice cream," I say. "Afterwards, do you want to see where I grew up?"

"Let's go," she says.

After taking V to Dairy Queen, I drive her to my family's first government-subsidized fourplex in Fridley, then the fourplex and duplex we had after that. I still remember the layouts of every place I've ever lived, so I tell V what they were like on the inside. I also talk about the teasing I took on the bus when I was picked up at these places, and what it was like to sometimes have to rely on food shelves for the next meal.

As we pull into our current house, the extreme contrast is hard to ignore — for both of us. I think about how this situation is an ongoing challenge for me and all parents. We want our kids to have a better life than we did, and we'll do anything for them. But we also don't want to spoil them or insulate them from the real world. All I can do is talk to V about gratitude and hope she'll remember this day as clearly as I will.

Childhood is a challenging time for everyone, regardless of your background. I've had my share of hardships, but I didn't have to deal with a pandemic, social unrest, political polarization and the "comparison" pressures that social media has inflicted on kids today, especially girls.

Parenting is also incredibly complex. There's no guide you can follow to get it perfect. I'm not saying I have it all figured out. I definitely don't. All I know is that we need to keep getting better and keep taking care of each other. We all need to put the devices down, be in the present and always keep our arms wide open.

Acknowledgments

I RECENTLY HEARD a speaker say one of the most interesting things I've ever heard: "The next time you look in a mirror, ask yourself, 'Whose faces do I see in my own?' Then ask, 'Who sees my face in theirs?'"

That's how I feel when I think of everyone who played a role in telling this story. There are the people who helped me put this specific book together. Then there's the enormous list of friends, family, mentors, coaches and colleagues who shaped my life and created the individual stories I've just shared.

To everyone who has helped me go on an incredible journey that's still just getting started, know that I see all of your faces. Thank you for being part of my life and allowing me to be a part of yours. A special thanks to Marc Conklin for encouraging me to tell my personal story and helping me get it all on paper. Thanks to Gina for being by my side during some of the craziest years leading up to this book, and for continuing to be there. Thanks to Gina's amazing daughter, Gianna, for being so engaged in this project and always taking the time to offer her insights.

And most of all, thanks to V for continuing to be my primary source of inspiration. V, I see your face in everything I do!

Opportunities

In addition to speaking and mentoring, I'm always eager to explore partnerships with entrepreneurs, and invest in or acquire other companies. If you'd like to explore these opportunities with me, visit ConnectwithKL.com or scan the QR code below.

www.ingramcontent.com/pod-product-compliance
Lightning Source LLC
Chambersburg PA
CBHW060925120626
46557CB00003B/877